STUDIES IN MODERN

GERMAN LITERATURE

STUDIES IN MODERN

GERMAN LITERATURE

SUDERMANN · HAUPTMANN · WOMEN WRITERS OF
THE NINETEENTH CENTURY

OTTO HELLER, PH.D.

Essay Index Reprint Series

BOOKS FOR LIBRARIES PRESS, INC.
FREEPORT, NEW YORK

First published 1905
Reprinted 1967

830.9
H 36 s
6 5 5 1 7
April 1969

LIBRARY OF CONGRESS CATALOG CARD NUMBER:

67-26748

PRINTED IN THE UNITED STATES OF AMERICA

TO

M. S. H.

THIS VOLUME IS AFFECTIONATELY

DEDICATED

PREFACE

The reader of these studies will be likely to feel a certain disappointment at finding them distinctly unscholastic in form as well as in substance. Yet a frank declaration of the author's aim may vindicate him in the judgment even of those who have themselves dealt with similar subjects in a more academic fashion. His cardinal purpose has been to draw attention afresh to a phase of contemporary culture thus far not sufficiently heeded by the English-speaking world. He has written with the hope of coöperating, in however modest a measure, with abler and better known writers who are striving to bring the German and the American into more genuine sympathy with each other.

The usual way of revealing the spirit and temper of a people through their literature is by an interpretative survey of the entire output. This course, if applied to modern literatures, involves the application of historical method to present-day things and persons. Many critics have deemed their powers adequate to grapple with such an enormous difficulty. But although they have had the advantage of an already well-informed reading public, their performances, as a rule, have fallen so far short of their aims that a less self-assured reviewer shrinks from the undertaking. With the exception of one or two brilliant achievements, the existing works of the sort render at most the limited service of *catalogues raisonnés*, — arranging the facts with different degrees of reliability, and tracing with more or less fallibility the general drift of modern, or, better, recent, literature. For an alien reader, unacquainted with the material under discussion, they are ill adapted. The novice naturally enough is much more interested in the æsthetic and ethical maxims of leading individuals and their concrete works than in any abstract creeds and doctrines of the schools. But the "history" of literature, or even of single literary periods, necessarily depends for the characterization of eminent writers upon condensed synopses and brief and usually dogmatic estimates, while for the expounding of the sociological bases from which literary currents ever spring, it must fall back on comment which for the greater part lies beyond the ken of all but the specialist.

Withal the historical method in this field of work is hardly safer from the danger of subjective treatment than is a more frankly "impressionistic" form of criticism. So soon as the "general" reader turns for confirmation of its verdicts to the full bench of critical authority, he is confused by a diversity of opinion which extends even to the estimates of the master spirits of the age. Like less imposing mortals, the historiographer of contemporary events cannot get away from his own shadow.

The author of this book, not unconscious of the subjective warp in his own judgment, has considered it more
to his purpose to show in a series of unconstrained mono-
graphs the chief aspects of modern German literature
than to construct a general guidebook for that subject.
By dint of detailed analysis he has sought to convey
the gist of the two leading writers even to such of his
readers as might be debarred from first-hand acquaintance with them.

Just why Hauptmann and Sudermann were chosen to
represent the modern tendencies in the drama and in
fiction is stated fully in the early part of the first sketch.
The paper on Women Writers of the Nineteenth Century,
although broader in scope and consequently less intensive
in treatment, was joined to those on Sudermann and
Hauptmann for the simple reason that it seemed practical to select out of the fullness of the available material
just those topics which for people outside of Germany
possess the keenest actuality. Should this beginning
prove not altogether abortive, it is the author's intention
to follow up the present volume with further groups
of studies, and he even hopes by this means to round
out, less unmethodically than would appear at first blush,
the story of the growth, ascendency, and, if signs may
be believed, the decline, of naturalism in German literature under the new Empire.

As for the style, or, should that be a misnomer, the
linguistic make-up, of these studies, the author, alas,

may not appease the sternly disposed among his readers with rueful promises of future improvement. Yet the much-tried leniency extended to writers, whether alien born or not, by a public with whom this form of generosity amounts almost to a national fault, relieves him of the need for prolonged apology.

OTTO HELLER

May, 1905

CONTENTS

MODERN
GERMAN LITERATURE

HERMANN SUDERMANN

HERMANN SUDERMANN

It is a striking coincidence that the most significant figures in the history of German literature have appeared upon the scene two by two. As far back as the ninth century we find side by side as its greatest poetic monuments two religious epopees of almost equal importance, the *Heliand* and the *Evangelienbuch;* among the popular epics of the Hohenstaufen times the German Iliad, the *Nibelungenlied*, is matched off by the *Lay of Kudrun* as by a German Odyssey; and among the chivalric poems of the same period the preeminent works of Wolfram von Eschenbach and Gottfried von Strassburg lend expression to diametrically opposite views of life.

After the literary life had lain in catalepsy for many generations it was reawakened in the eighteenth century through apparently antipodal forces which may perhaps be most fitly brought to mind by the mention of Klopstock and Lessing. Then the dazzling flood of light and life which at the close of that century suffused the culture of Germany was shed from the twin luminaries Goethe

3

and Schiller. For the people, even to-day the
name of Goethe hardly enjoys the same lonely emi-
nence in German letters as does Homer's in Greek
or Shakespeare's in English literature. Although
in the ensuing century the catalogue of the *poetae
Germaniae* grew to an unexampled magnitude, its
best known names at successive periods stood in
contrasted couples: Kleist and Körner, Uhland
and Hauff, Heine and Lenau, Geibel and Freilig-
rath, Grillparzer and Hebbel, Reuter and Scheffel, Freytag and Keller, Heyse and Spielhagen,
Wilbrandt and Wildenbruch, Marlitt and Werner,
and, if the truth must be confessed, Hackländer
and Gerstäcker. We are therefore not surprised
to find ourselves once more contrasting two leaders
— this time within the *Moderne*. Now that the
new school has issued from its turbulent infancy
it has become legitimate for us to ask: What
have these new writers done for German literature, — in what have they enriched the national
art and culture? To the great mass of the people the literature of the post-Bismarckian era
seems epitomized in two names,— Gerhart Hauptmann and Hermann Sudermann, for undeniably
these two have exercised the greatest formative
influence on contemporaneous German letters.

Literary criticism, ever inclined to juxtaposition
and antithesis, has quickly adopted the dualism
of the public taste in its attitude toward Sudermann and Hauptmann.

To trace out the artistic and intellectual growth
of these two leading spirits as manifest in their
works is an attractive and instructive task. To
be sure, their careers show in the main features a
certain external similarity, a similarity which has
been strikingly emphasized through the circumstance that they have been simultaneously swept
onward to the very pinnacle of fame. Yet though
their great successes have very nearly tallied in
point of time and measure, one can scarcely im-
agine two more dissimilar natures. Scherer's
ingenious but somewhat strained theory which
accounts for the main tendencies of German literature through the underlying competition of rival
forces, a masculine and a feminine, is well illus-
trated in these two writers. Hauptmann, high-
strung, responding with nervous sensibility to the
mildest stimulus, is possessed of a reproductive,
feminine talent, a talent raised, to be sure, to the
power of genius; whereas Sudermann is a robust
masculine personality made of coarser stuff, not
subtle enough to penetrate the inmost privacies

of the human heart. Withal he is not the lesser
artist, for to offset Hauptmann's fineness of perception he has the advantage of a stout self-confi-
dence and broad knowledge of the inner and outer
facts of life.

The fame of Hermann Sudermann is no longer
confined to his own country, since most of his
novels have been translated into several languages
and a number of his plays performed in the more
dignified theaters on both sides of the Atlantic.
His successes, won in the face of a determined
opposition both from the old school of writers and
the new,—since neither will acknowledge Sudermann as of their own,—have been phenomenal, and,
if the question can be decided by the evidence of
publishers' and library statistics and the frequency
of Sudermann's plays in the repertory of leading
theaters, it may be safely assumed that his present
great popularity is in no danger of decline in the
near future. This popularity is unquestionably
connected with the fact that in each of his works
a living issue is sharply defined. Sudermann is
above all things a writer with a distinct pedagogical task to which he brings a complete intellectual and moral equipment. His bold and positive
utterances have awakened a ringing echo, because

they have imperatively called the attention of the world to social and intellectual undercurrents of extraordinary persistency and unknown power.

To determine one's attitude toward the upsetting doctrine preached by Sudermann, with the approval of a large portion of the best lettered and intellectually most fastidious of living nations, would seem to be almost a duty for the thoughtful. If the code of ethics he accepts and proclaims is asserted with justice to be a source of peril to the vested social order that most of us would defend, is it not the part of wisdom to measure the danger by looking the enemy manfully in the face? New thoughts are not killed off when fine indignation virtuously conspires to smother them in their cradle. In a free country it is worth while to examine new teachings. As for those of Sudermann, most Americans will gasp at their import and unhesitatingly reject them, yet few readers, if they study his books to a purpose, will refuse their respect to the sincerity and moral earnestness of the man.

It shall be the aim of this chapter to discuss the works thus far produced by Hermann Sudermann, —to review their chief contents and trace out their ethics, marking with heavier lines those features which have divided the opinion of the German public. But since a fruit of experience is caution, the execution of this plan needs to be preceded by a word of explanation. People often do the critic the unintentional honor of holding him accountable for the views of the eminent writers whom he expounds, only because, out of sheer respect for his readers as well as his subject, he modestly abstains from the promulgation of any personal theory of life that he may hold. To all eventual charges of heresy and sedition the defense therefore enters a general plea of "not guilty." The writer does not pose as Hermann Sudermann nor as his keeper. He does not necessarily champion Sudermann's ethics simply because he does not consider it his business forever to make war upon them. It is enough for him to sound this rich personality, to communicate its message, and to furnish thereby, if he may allow himself the hope, some food for serious reflection.

The German people have displayed in their literature as a whole a certain severity of temper. Where this literature runs in a humorous vein it passes easily into rough persiflage and cutting satire. Satire is the dominant note not only in the bulky controversial literature of the sixteenth

century but also in a not inconsiderable portion
of the classic writings of the eighteenth. Lessing's critical activity, sublimely constructive
though it is, is pervaded by rankling animosity
against every form of intellectual sloth and
artistic barrenness. The youthful Goethe directs
his boyishly harsh censure against the prevailing
vices of philistinism and hypocrisy. Schiller, in
his youth still more vehement than either of his
two great predecessors, hurls bowlderlike invec-
tive against the existing political and social order
of things. The Romantics, priding themselves on
their greater delicacy of feeling, seek to refine
satire into the gentler art of irony. But even
among them it never dies out in its poignant form.
In the period of reaction "Young Germany"
resorts to merciless scorn as the only weapon
available against despotism. Ludwig Börne and
Heinrich Heine are the greatest satirists of
"Young Germany." They deal havoc differently,
— the shafts of Börne's sarcasm hit and pierce,
while those of Heine's touch and poison. Later
on Friedrich Theodor Vischer, the famous writer
on æsthetics, subjects his German countrymen to
Aristophanic censure in his *Faust, the Third
Part of the Tragedy*. And that entire faction

who are commonly designated as " Youngest
Germany," or *Die Moderne*, are fain, in order it
may be to facilitate their analysis, to saturate
the actualities of modern life with a corrosive
mockery. Although a certain realism usually
serves as the basis of satire, it is the nature of
satire to overstep the literal truth. In order to
show up a thing as deserving our contempt or
ridicule authors present a distorted picture of it.
Thus the realism which obtains in caricature is
one which depends less on correspondence to
facts than on suggestive association. The satirist, be his love of truth never so great, seeks not
to present things just as they really appear to
him from without, but to draw a convincing likeness of that which they suggest to his inward
experience. This object he achieves by exagger-
ating or overaccentuating their sinister or mean
aspects. He retouches the picture of reality, but
never for the purpose of embellishment or ideal-
ization. These distinctions it is necessary to hold
fast in order to understand why the most distinguished living satirist, — Hermann Sudermann,
— although he has been so often called modern
from top to toe, is at most a half-hearted " realist."
He does not conform to the naturalist's supreme

demand that the writer must not permit his
personality, and above all things his philosophy,
to shine through his work. On the contrary, it
is not at all difficult to get a satisfying glimpse
of the man Sudermann through the medium of
his writings. He is a typical modern man, city
bred, sagacious, and sophisticated to a degree,
knowing the world so thoroughly that few things
in it can baffle, puzzle, or even surprise him.
Such, I think, is the first impression formed of
him. Next we observe the open-mindedness of
the man, the broad liberality of his sympathies.
Soon we discover that his cosmopolitanism has
in no way denationalized him or, as is apt to be
the case, made him an utter worldling. For with
his world-citizenship is coupled a strong family
feeling for the German land and people and
a deep religious sense. Sudermann, in these
days of national self-assertion and spiritual path-
seeking, is neither a scoffer nor an indifferent.
His skepticism does not assail any noble human
ideals, for by these he is himself deeply inspired;
but he is distrustful of men's motives, and especially of the stereotyped moral notions unthink-
ingly accepted by one generation from the other.
Morality — one may so interpret Sudermann —

must be earned, not inherited; personally differentiated, not typified. How a person wins or loses his moral salvation is the problem whose fascination sets Sudermann to work, for, although a doubter by temperament, he clearly perceives in human nature latent moral forces which if set free will let it rise above the stale, warmed-over morality of workaday life. It follows naturally that a writer of this temper should be concerned with a dual purpose, — rudely to shake the decaying structure of social morality now resting largely on hollow conventions and compromises, but at the same time to stay the total collapse of society and invigorate it with his own sustaining aspirations. As his attempts toward these ends are not wholly free from theatricalities, the unthinking complaint that Sudermann is a *poseur* has passed into the stock in trade of contemporary criticism. He does not parade his personality, he is simply not quite artist enough always to hide it. To be sure, a few of his characters, notably Count Trast in *Die Ehre*, have a strong affinity with Sudermann himself. Yet they were never intended for self-portraits. In fact, not caring to admit the throng into his intimacy, he rather barricades himself defiantly behind his works. From this

position he falls savagely upon that painted, slinking, day-shunning society which for him is the
object of deep detestation and drags it from the
privacy of its nocturnal haunts into the pitiless
glare of the sunlit street. Sudermann, then, is
and can be no dreamy minstrel nor yet an utterer
of the "lyric cry." He is a calculating man of
action, a self-conscious altruist agitated by deepest sympathy for all souls that are in distress and
by implacable hatred of every form of tyranny.
Fortunately this determined judge and resolute
avenger is also an artist of uncommon power.
His plays belong probably, his novels beyond a
doubt, to the best that German literature has to
show in these genres.

Before Hermann Sudermann leaped into fame
through the performance of *Die Ehre* (at the Lessing Theater in Berlin, November 27, 1889) he had
struggled with hardships in obscurity, support-
ing himself variously as a private tutor, journalist,
and story-writer for — family magazines! He was
born in 1857, the son of a brewer in a small village of East Prussia, where brewers are not *ex
officio* millionaires. Sudermann's father, in greatly
straitened circumstances, contrived to maintain the
talented boy at school with a brief interruption,

during which the fourteen-year-old Hermann shared by force of poverty the early fate of Ibsen and Fontane in being apprenticed to an apothecary. Returning to his books, Sudermann was graduated from the Gymnasium at Tilsit, and then undertook work in philology and history at the University of Königsberg. In 1877 he came to Berlin to continue his studies and has since then made the Prussian capital his permanent home. His importance as a leader in the modern literary movement dates properly from the year 1887, when, besides a collection of short stories entitled *Im Zwielicht* (" In the Gloaming "), he produced his first work of real significance, the novel *Frau Sorge* ("Dame Care"), which revealed him at once as a writer of exceptional force and skill and also as a mature philosopher.

" Dame Care " is a somber book. The hero is a man who has led a joyless existence. He has never been young, since upon his early childhood wretched parental strife had sprinkled its poisoning mildew. The beginning reads not very unlike Reuter's great book, *Ut mine Stromtid;* but how different is Reuter's noble portrait of Carl Havermann from the picture drawn of Paul Mayhöfer's father, the East Prussian squire, who, uprooted from his easy mode of life, thenceforth spins out his days in apathetic stupor! Young Paul, who assumes all the obligations of his bankrupt father, is not only borne down with the weight of excessive exertions, but burdened also with the still heavier responsibility for the moral safety of his family. After the death of his mother no ray of light ever pierces the veil which, woven by Dame Care, is drawing closer and closer round the slow, shy, and rather unwinsome boy. Cheerlessly, almost mechanically, he performs his monotonous work, in order to provide comfort for the father now sinking into dotage and the reckless twin sisters. Success crowns Paul's labors; but no sooner has the lost credit of his name been recovered through untiring labor than it is again disgraced in a still more painful manner. To repair the damaged honor of his sisters is a sacred debt which Paul owes to the memory of his mother. After summoning up in vain the full measure of his moral heroism for an appeal to the seducers, he intimidates the cowards with a brutal threat and forces them to make good their promises of marriage. But after this one resolute, blood-cleansing deed he relapses into dull, oxlike resignation. His business prospers more and more, but to no purpose, since now the sisters are married, and Paul is no longer buoyed up by his guardianship. He is enslaved by a false, a cheerless conception of life. It must be said that the road by which he ultimately reaches liberty takes a most incongruous course, for it leads through the penitentiary. In order to preserve the property of a neighbor from the incendiary hands of his degenerate father, Paul sets his own premises on fire, and having thus reduced himself to poverty, he must in addition atone for his act by two years of penal servitude. When at last he steps from his prison the love of a true woman awaits him at the gates, seeking him out with a happiness that he had been too awkward to pursue. This solution of the psychologic problem is not satisfying because it does not appear as inevitable. From the gray web of Phantom Care why did not Paul extricate himself for good, when, pistol in hand, he set his face against the defilers of his home? Sundry other technical objections might be raised against Sudermann's first famous novel; but in spite of its faults, *Frau Sorge* is among the noblest works of modern German fiction. This is not saying that it is a book to be recommended without caution. As a keen and fearless scrutinizer, Sudermann naturally draws into the sphere of his novels some discussions not intended for the ears of the "young miss," or of her worthy progenitor utterly indisposed to endure in fiction the undeniable facts of life. The careful parent does not always remember that the young person in question has already a considerable library of her own. Sudermann is not a competitor of Mmes. Wildermuth, Polko, and Heimburg in Germany, or in America of the manufacturers of such brummagem historical fiction as *Richard Carvel* and *The Crisis*, or in England of the writers of such unliterary trash as *The Prisoner of Zenda*. Of this, new evidence is furnished in *Die Geschwister* ("Brothers and Sisters"), two tales published in 1888, in both of which the same problem is handled. In the first story, *Geschichte einer stillen Mühle* ("History of a Lonely Mill"), one brother loves the wife of the other. The tragedy is heightened by the deep attachment the wrongdoer feels for the wronged, and it ends with their common death. The second story deals with the growing passion of a girl for her sister's husband; for one moment she gives room to a wish for the invalid sister's death, and for this platonic crime she voluntarily pays with

her own life. The right of untrammeled liberty, it
will be noticed, is not asserted. The moral code
is sustained by the tragic issue as firmly as in
Goethe's *Die Wahlverwandtschaften*, to which the
story bears a certain inner resemblance. But no
insipid matrimonial amity is preached when the
ill-starred heroine Olga speaks in defiance of the
convention as follows: "I should love differently
from you two; I should not be faint-hearted; I
should not sneak away as you do saying, ''T is better thus.' I should subdue her with the fire of my
soul, vanquish her with the strength of my arms.
I should snatch her to my breast and carry her off,
no matter whither, out into the night, into the
desert, if no sun were willing to shine for us, no
house to offer its shelter. I would rather starve
with her by the roadside than ask the slightest
favor of the world that would separate us. This
is what I should do if I were you, Robert. And
if I were she, I should throw myself on your breast
laughing, and say, ' Come, I will beg for you when
you are without bread, my lap shall be your couch
when you are without a bed, your wounds I will
bathe with my tears, a thousand deaths I will suffer for you and thank the Lord that He permits
me.' See, Robert, this is my idea of love."

Reserving Sudermann's epoch-marking play *Die Ehre* ("Honor") for discussion in connection with the other dramas, we turn to his next novel.

Der Katzensteg (in the English translation "Regina") (1889) is a great book in nearly every sense. Among its many distinctive merits it teaches us to appreciate a profound historic sense in this true son of the modern era. The action is laid in the year 1814. With a distrustful eye Sudermann subjects that glorious chapter of German history to a thorough scrutiny. Unbribed by the verdict of patriotic tradition or by his own strong instinctive love of his country, he scans the records of the past. And he finds his misgivings confirmed. A sad disillusionment indeed, and a heavy blow for many a patriotic soul. "That year," — he says, as a result of his unprejudiced investigation, — "that year whose name rings in the ears of us children of a later day like one grand harmony woven of pæans, organ peals, and the clanging of bells, witnessed more violence and crime than any other year before or since."

As has been said, the tragedy is brought to a head in the glorious year 1814, but it was engendered fully seven years before. In 1807 Napoleon had subdued Prussia; the Baron von Schranden, a Prussian nobleman who from his mother's breast had imbibed Polish sympathies, now seeing in the rising star of Bonaparte a gleam of hope for his beloved Poland, at the prompting of this hope becomes guilty of high treason. A French detachment being quartered in his castle, Schranden forces the fifteen-year-old Regina Hackelberg, as an obedient tool of his felony, to guide the French troops over the so-called *Katzensteg* ("cat's trail") up to the rear of the Prussians. These, suddenly attacked, are massacred to a man. When the facts come out, a savage wrath rises up against the baron. His castle is stormed and burned by the furious peasants. On his crumbling manor he lives henceforth in dismal isolation. Mantraps and spring guns barely safeguard his life; from all communion with men he is banished. He is an outlawed man. Nobody will or dares work for him, and his estates are of no use to him. But two more victims are doomed through his crime: Regina, who remains with the baron, his drudge and mistress, and Schranden's son Boleslav, at school in Königsberg, who finds himself suddenly avoided by all his associates. He leaves the school as soon as he learns the reason, and under an assumed name enters the corps of Lützow's famous volunteers in the warfare against the French. But the curse has fastened itself to him. The arrival of a former chum causes him to decamp for fear of discovery. He next joins a militia regiment, is wounded in a most hazardous war adventure, held prisoner, and at last, when peace has been made, returns to his home. At this point begins the story of Regina. Boleslav's father has just died, and the villagers refuse decent burial to his body. Arriving on the scene, Boleslav finds Regina in the act of digging a grave. Schooled in rigid self-discipline, and in his misfortune upheld by unflinching self-respect and a lofty sense of duty, he sees in Regina only the vile accomplice of the wretch for whom he has come to perform the last filial office. He accordingly treats her with rude contempt. His comrades in arms have come at his call to help him inter his father, but they leave him in ominous silence as soon as the business is over. Then Boleslav is brought face to face with the awfulness of his future fate: "And his hand will be against every man, and every man's hand against him." While waiting to decide about his future, he tolerates Regina and allows her to minister to his wants, which she does with a brutelike attachment. Soon touched by her supreme self-oblivion, he feels himself more and more attracted by the native charm of the strange creature, who through self-surrendering obedience was beguiled into shame and crime in early years, and yet has preserved intact her truest character, unswerving loyalty and chaste dignity. Quelling his wakening passion for her, Boleslav throws himself into his work. Intrepid he stands, in single-handed defiance of the patriotic mob. Patriots indeed they who show their teeth and foam at the mouth in their frantic eagerness to punish the third, nay even the fourth, generation for every affront offered their hollow idols! A true hero, he routs the cowardly pack, and strives and strains and slaves to win back his own in the teeth of persecution, until the blast of the war trumpet is heard once more. Without a moment's hesitation, as though it were the only natural course of action, he throws to the winds the fruit of his herculean efforts, responds to the call of his country, and after burying Regina, who has laid down her life for his, dies an obscure but glorious death for his fatherland.

It is readily seen, even from this bare outline, that *Der Katzensteg* is strongly touched up with

romantic tints; a fuller study would make it
equally evident that in spite of the thrilling interest in the story as such, and the gusto with
which the figures and their setting are treated
on their own account, *Der Katzensteg* is also a
vigorous sermon, as all of Sudermann's books are
in their last analysis. The theme of this sermon
is patriotism, true and false. Only once again,
in the one-act play *Teja*, does Sudermann glorify
the genuine patriotic spirit. There, as in *Der
Katzensteg*, patriotism appears but as a necessary
phase of the categorical imperative which dictates
the conduct of the hero. What greater contrast
could be imagined than that between Boleslav,
who, martyred by the gross injustice of society,
upholds and defends the sacredness of his manly
duties towards that same society, and Hauptmann's self-seeking, self-losing Master Heinrich,
who sacrifices all society, even his own family,
to the chimera of a duty towards himself or his
fancied genius.

Sudermann's next novel is neither romantic
nor is it a "novel with a purpose." The breezy
story of *Iolanthes Hochzeit* (" The Wedding of
Iolanthe ") (1892) is generally underrated, largely
because narrative art is not in itself sufficiently

appreciated by Germans (nor, for the matter of that, by Americans). Readers are apt to value a story wholly for the incident; and in this respect *Iolanthes Hochzeit* does not offer anything that is striking. It tells how a grim old bachelor makes a belated and abortive attempt at matrimony. He is no sooner married than he is so panic-stricken at the changed aspect of life that on the evening of his wedding day he solemnly betroths his newly acquired wife to the other man in the case; and then he rubs his hands in Mephistophelian glee over his singular disencumberment from the roseate chains so irksome in the very anticipation. Surely the plot is slight. Yet Sudermann has succeeded in fashioning out of the meager story a cabinet piece of vernacular art worthy of a Fritz Reuter. The right note has been happily struck from the first and it is sustained to the end. The story is fairly redolent with the racy savor of provincial life in the north of Germany. Sudermann has never been excelled in his portraiture of the most singular product of East Prussia; I mean the *Krautjunker* or country squire, a puzzling mixture of thick-headedness and jovial humor, generosity and crude bigotry, caste conceit and patriotic devotion, materialism and stanch

belief in ideals. This novel fully reveals along
with Sudermann's well-known critical tendency
the dramatic bent of his narrative. Somewhat
surprising from this master of scathing sarcasm
is the subtle irony that hovers over the narrative
like an ethereal gauze.

In judging of Sudermann's next novel, *Es War*
("Once upon a Time") (1894), which in some
respects is inferior to "Dame Care" and "Regina,"
it ought to be remembered that it was written
fully ten years before publication. It too, nevertheless, gives ample evidence of the author's
extraordinary faculties and forces, which have
contributed in equal shares to its excellence.
For the better understanding of the book, a limitation needs now to be put on the statement that
Sudermann is a pessimist. Pessimism appears
plainly enough in his analysis and diagnosis of
things, yet far is it from him to look into the
future through smoke-bedimmed spectacles. He
does not view the moral attainments of the living
generation with contentment. But his belief in
the transmission of character is not that of the
determinist, and he does not believe uncondition-
ally in the power of the past over the future. A
guilt committed cannot be undone, to be sure,

yet a strong will may come out victorious in the
fight with the threatening consequences of past
error. This, however, cannot be through remorse,
so Sudermann teaches. Like Nietzsche, he casts
sterile repentance overboard. The world can be
moved not by tears but by deeds. Only it is
needful — and this is the central lesson of the
novel *Es War* — that a man break with his guilty
past irrevocably by unqualified, fearless, and
unsparing avowal. In *Es lebe das Leben* ("The
Joy of Living"), act iii, scene vii, Richard,
in his perplexity, exclaims: "Ah, Beate! Truth,
Truth! To be once more at peace with oneself!
For the bare privilege of having a conviction I
would throw down joyfully everything, my paltry
private existence, my life — everything." A man
must make a clean sweep of his past if he would
recover the mastery of his fate. Not until the
hero of *Es War* learns to understand this can
he redeem himself, make good the past as far as
that is ever possible, and become again an active
man. Leo Sellenthin is one of those broad-chested
giants, ruthlessly egoistic and full of go, whom
we meet frequently in Sudermann's works. An
affair of honor in which his part has been that of
the doubly guilty offender and slayer takes him

to America, whence he is drawn back by the characteristic attachment of the East Elbian to his native heath. At home again, he meets the companion of his past wrong, now the wife of his most devoted friend. Leo himself is responsible for the ill-fated union, for when Felicitas' present husband, disquieted by rumors, once put the direct question, Leo lied away his liaison with her. Now he is lured back by the unprincipled wretch, loses his poise and self-respect entirely, and, in his own words, is fast going "to the dogs," till finally the woman, exasperated at his resolve that they shall die together, precipitates an explanation between Leo and her wronged husband. The issue does not result in the usual exchange of pistol formalities so gratifying to the logic of the habitual novel reader, for Ulrich, with a magnanimity quite unbecoming a German gentleman and an officer, pardons his "friend." On the German Becky Sharp's fair shoulders falls all the punishment, whereas Leo strides out afresh into a future promiseful of fortune and love. To our ethical conceptions the end is far from satisfying, but Sudermann — and this dogmatism constitutes one of his weaknesses — is bound to prove a thesis. His characters may fitly be divided into two

classes: the active or potent, and the passive or
impotent, — the driving and the drifting. To the
former goes out the writer's approval, regardless
of fine moral distinctions; to the latter, his sympathy, pity, blame, or contempt. In order to compel Sudermann's respect a man must, above all
things, possess an imperturbable individuality, an
ego of his own making. There is at least nothing mysterious, nothing unpractical, in this robust
doctrine.

The same idea is preached in Sudermann's plays
even more emphatically and drastically than in his
novels. Most of these plays are social plays, even
as the novels were social novels. With fists of
iron they hammer at the bars of the protecting
fence which the old use-and-wont of society has
drawn round its ancient structure. If in *Frau
Sorge* and in *Es War* the great satirist has
wielded a scourge, he chastens with scorpions in
Die Ehre (" Honor "), in *Heimat* (called in the
English translation " Magda "), and in *Sodoms
Ende* (" The Destruction of Sodom "). In turning
our interest to these and the other problem plays,
let us bear in mind that behind the dramatis personæ in them stand living social questions of our
time. To show the common ground from which

the conflicts spring in his dramas, the means
by which they are driven to a climax, and, lastly,
the method by which they reach solution, is the
purpose of the following epitome of Sudermann's
social philosophy. Sudermann sees in human
society not a firm conglomerate, but rather,
as it were, a stratified formation of which each
layer is a separate world in miniature. To him
the eternal warfare of human interests is thus
a struggle between contiguous strata of society.
Whether the war be waged between the aristocracy and the middle class, or between the
propertied class and the proletariat, or whether
the parties to the conflict be the employer and the
employed, the producer and the middleman, the
soldier and the civilian, or lastly, to use a term
become famous through Sudermann, the front-
house folk and the rear-house folk, there is, in
all these cases, a necessary contact of some sort
which causes friction. The insularity of the social
groups is even greater than this fact alone would
explain. For each caste in its intimate soul life
stands solitary, not only over against the adjacent,
but over against every other caste. It cannot
understand the others and is not understood by
them. It is perfectly true, as the veteran novelist

Spielhagen urges, that this is not a new discovery; but who before Sudermann had ever clearly made it the thesis of a play?

Now it often happens that an exceptional individual in the course of developing his superior gifts steps beyond the circle assigned him by the accident of birth. Woe betide such a man if the severance of the ties that hold him to his native circle be incomplete, if by a sense of duty and piety he retain allegiance to the narrower province, and if habit and family affection stay the hand that would burst its own shackles! To conclude from these premises that Sudermann's warning finger points the way back for him who has strayed from his home would be misinterpreting his central lesson. On the contrary, he urges *déclassés* of this sort unmistakably to the path that leads to freedom. In his earlier works, at least, he cares more for the individual than for the social group; and his favorite hero seems to be the person who fights for the higher place for which he is fitted.

The drift of Sudermann's first drama, *Die Ehre* ("Honor") (1890; performed November, 1889), which brought him sudden fame, opposes the common sentiment that honor is a supreme ideal possession in which all men can share; more in

particular, the play goes to refute the prevalent
German notions upon the subject of personal
honor. Count Trast, the counseling friend of
the leading character, who would drive out that
phantom and have men's conduct ruled instead
by a high sense of justice, probably articulates the
author's ethics in branding conventional honor as
one of the conventional lies. It is perhaps not
without a deep significance that on the stage the
distinguished cosmopolite bears a marked external
resemblance to the author. At any rate, Trast is
not really and seriously bound up with the plot,
and serves in the main only to promulgate the
above-sketched philosophy, which task he accom-
plishes by a flow of eloquence richly besprinkled
with bonmots. Our sympathies are won, in greater
measure even than by his rôle as Robert Heinecke's mentor, by the precious manner in which
he plays havoc with the vacuous Kurt Mühlingk
and his boon companions, and at no stage is he
so sure of our applause as when amid sardonic
laughter he rakes the fashionable young libertines
over the undying coals of his satire. Throughout
the play Trast creates the impression that the playwright himself has in this thin disguise mounted
the stage and is moving with characteristic aplomb

among his own creatures. This importance of
Count Trast as the exponent of Sudermann's
philosophy makes it proper, though he is not
the hero, to speak of him before all the other
characters of *Die Ehre*. When a mere stripling
of a lieutenant he was discharged *mit schlichtem
Abschied*, i.e. he left the regiment under a cloud.
The reason was a by no means uncommon one.
The trouble had grown out of his inability to
pay a gambling debt on short order, but the
real crime was that he declined the brotherly
invitation to make use of a loaded pistol which a
committee of his fellow-officers had generously
provided for his suicide. Now after a lapse of
time he comes back, an Indian "coffee king" of
vast wealth and commercial influence. The tri-
fling debt of ninety thousand thalers he has long
ago discharged, without in the slightest degree
reinstating himself in the good graces of his own
father, much less rehabilitating himself with the
exclusive coterie to which he formerly belonged.
A checkered experience has taught him not only
to look beyond the restricted horizons of his
former and his present social positions, but also
to shake himself free of every class prejudice
whatsoever. He is a completed *Lebenskünstler*,

a past master in the art of living, a man who, like Goethe's *Wilhelm Meister*, has at last learned to shape circumstances to his own needs instead of allowing himself to be shaped by them, has learned to be the hammer rather than the anvil in the forge of life. In the portrayal of this imposing personage Sudermann furnishes proof that with all his congenital love for his fatherland he is in truth a citizen of that larger home which is not defined on the map with colored inks. This is revealed in Trast's rare freedom from the provincialism which insistently crops out in Germans in ever so many little ways, even if they have traveled. Trast is first and last a man of the world, equally at his ease with the German merchant and the Indian Rajah, in the London club and the continental Casino, amid the gayety of the Latin Quarter of Paris and the busy hubbub of downtown New York. It has been stated that before justice this man bows as to his ruling power; he recognizes no other moral law. Naturally he makes strong enemies. But he is callously indifferent to public opinion. As a rule he is let alone, because he keeps disagreeable persons at a distance with a tone and gesture which he holds in reserve for the purpose. For the rest he has perfect polish and self-control, is proud but not arrogant, always disposed to be considerate, but prone to vent his sarcasm, which is cutting and slightly cynical.

Under the tutelage of this well-balanced man, Robert Heinecke, the youthful hero of the play, has progressed considerably in worldly knowledge, though he still lacks the poise that is needed in his predicament. Sprung from very lowly stock, he has raised himself through signal ability and perseverance, not without the aid of favoring fortune, to an important mercantile position. After many years of tireless work in the service of his former benefactor Kommerzienrat Mühlingk, Robert has just returned to Berlin from the Indian branch of the firm. Through all these years abroad how deeply has he yearned for his parents and sisters! On arriving, however, he feels at once, though he is slow to admit it to himself, that he has become unused to the spiritual atmosphere of his domestic circle. The chasm between Robert and his family is plainly hinted, in a cleverly casual way, through an episode in the first act. A manservant of the Mühlingks, who reside in the fronthouse (the Heineckes are living in the rear), has assumed a tone of insolent familiarity in delivering a message to young Heinecke. Robert's mother

invites the messenger to sit down with them:
"Won't you eat a piece of coffee-cake with us,
William? There is some left."

Robert: Pardon, mother (*he hands him a coin*);
the man has his pay. Say to the Herr Kommerzienrat that I hope he will do me the honor of
receiving me at one o'clock. I shall call at that
hour with the Count von Trast-Saarberg. (*Exit
the flunky.*)

Robert had come home without the slightest
suspicion of the state of things, though Trast had
forewarned him. Now as the truth begins to dawn
on him he has to listen to Trast's lecture: "Unhappy is the man who has fallen out of his caste
and has not the courage to cut loose his conscience
from it also." For each caste, according to Trast-
Sudermann, has a different morality, in particular
a special sense of honor. Robert learns to his horror that under the protectorate of her older sister,
the younger, Alma, has been maintaining illicit
but profitable relations with young Kurt Mühlingk.
In his first access of anger he demands from Kurt
the restitution of his family honor; but after a night
spent in tormenting sorrow his better judgment
prevails. He will lift his family out of the mire
and make for them a new home in some far-away

corner of the world. It is now that the vulgarity
of his family is brought home to Robert, and he
grows fully ashamed of the class with which birth
has thrown him, for he learns how comfortably
happy his nearest and dearest of kin feel in their
bottomless slough. The parents are blunted to a
true sense of their daughter's disgrace. Mühlingk
senior plasters their wounded honor with a good-
sized check, and Alma, but now threatened with
a melodramatic paternal curse, is overwhelmed
with clamorous gratitude by the honorable family
conclave. Her own matrimonial future lies bright
before her, since with her sinful fortune she has
now become a far better match than if her dowry
had consist-d of a complete assortment of the
womanly virtues. Robert can do no better than
turn his back on the despicable tribe. After a
stormy scene in the front-house, where he gives
a very *mauvais quart d'heure* to the Mühlingks,
father and son, he goes away, taking with him as
his bride Lenore, the noble-minded sister of Kurt.
This "heart-story," too palpably grafted on to the
stock of the play, is one of several complications
which are highly improbable and too plainly de-
signed for effect. On the whole, the motivation is
somewhat commonplace, and the exposition of the

Vorfabel, i.e. the action precedent to the play, rather violent. In its technic this play, which with its parallelism of corrupt wealth and corrupt poverty as in other respects is reminiscent of Anzengruber's *Das Vierte Gebot* (" The Fourth Commandment "), does not concert with the naturalistic movement which simultaneously with *Die Ehre* scored its first triumph in Hauptmann's "Before Sunrise." Monologue, that traditional makeshift of psychologic exposure, is not scorned, and even the notorious trick of "asides," so utterly discredited by the moderns, is employed in *Die Ehre,* which from its combining the methods of the French drama of the second empire with a greater realism has been properly termed a compromise play. The best merits of *Die Ehre* are its clever argumentation and the telling seizure of the *milieu.* But it is far inferior to later plays, and especially inadequate in its conclusion, which is brought on rather forcibly by that cleaver of all Gordian knots, the Count Trast-Saarberg. All the events make for a tragedy: it is averted by nothing but the good nature of the playwright and his *alter ego,* the inimitable count.

Much more "naturalistic" in its technic is Sudermann's second play, *Sodoms Ende* (" The

Destruction of Sodom ")(1891), a Juvenalian satire
on the wickedness of the modern Berlin. The
hero of this tragedy — if, remarks some German
critic, a wash-rag may even technically be termed
a hero — reminds us in some respects, notably in
his morbid incapacity for work, of Oswald Alving
in Ibsen's " Ghosts." A talented young fellow has
painted a picture dealing with the destruction of
Sodom, which more through its cynical candor
than by virtue of its intrinsic merit makes him
famous at a single stroke. There is in the play a
certain Dr. Weisse, who resembles in a perverted
way the celebrated Konrad Bolz in Freytag's *Die
Journalisten*, — a flaneur of much wit and clear
sight, but morally decrepit and inert. This man
remarks about the picture: " A thousand times
the subject has been worked, but in what fashion ?
In the foreground, on a rock, good Master Lot,
surrounded by other oxen and asses; a little farther
back his spouse, devotedly petrified into a pillar
of salt; and in the distance something which looks
like three burning matches !" Willy Janikow has
touched the tradition-worn subject with the flames
of his lurid fantasy; in his painting it becomes
the ghastly allegory of delirious sensuality and the
whirling chase after frantic pleasures. Such a

picture as that cannot fail to seize upon the fancy
of the Stock Exchange aristocracy for whom excitement and enjoyment are almost synonymous.
Accordingly, the *Tiergartenviertel*, always glad to
patronize that art which tugs hard at the nerve
cords, has received the new-fangled genius in its
lion cage and pampered and petted his considerable talent to death. Among us barbarians of the
West, with our still half-savage notions about the
superfluousness of art, such treatment does not
come to an aspiring artist. Nor need any American artist — I mean a real artist, not an artificer
— sigh for the hardening discipline of public indifference. In a city like St. Louis or Chicago the
ingenious Willy would, in all probability, have
gone through a protracted and rather inconvenient
régime of penury and semistarvation, instead of
falling into lassitude and luxurious ennui. Things
are different in Berlin, W. Dr. Weisse in his heyday fared equally well or ill: "Look at me! In
the province they call me a celebrity, and if you
open any newspaper you are sure to find my name.
One day I have been decorated with an order, another day a horse has run away with me — and
sundry other accidents of the sort. And yet I
am wretchedly gone to seed. My lyrics have all

vinegared this long time; no new ideas come to me." But he knows how to accommodate himself to the change: "So I have gone in for criticism. The howling dog has transformed himself into the biting dog." However, his pristine glory has departed: "Ah! what a great fellow I was in those days, when in every German bookcase the place of honor next to Henrietta Davidis' cookbook was reserved for me!" We know Sudermann's attitude towards such parasitic existences. In polar opposition to their moral apathy stands honest Professor Riemann, the sane and sober maker of fair to middling pictures, a man who closes his unspoiled heart hermetically against all wicked eccentricities. Riemann has no use for Nietzsche with his maxim, so alluring and convenient, of the "Beyond Good and Evil." "Let me alone with your gospel of vice, if you please," he remarks to the invertebrate Willy. In nearly every play of Sudermann some character seems to be authorized to speak for the author. Unquestionably Riemann in "The End of Sodom" is that special ablegate. Sudermann condones many sins in a man who, despite failures and downfalls, has at last attained a clarified, definite individuality; he esteems a powerful "Will to Live"; but his pity is as deaf for the

self-appointed "overman" as it is for the cry,
C'est plus fort que moi, — that eternal appeal of
the worm-eaten weakling. Sudermann is wholly
free from decadence. Although much obloquy
has been heaped on him for depicting such scandalous conditions and such a corrupt society as
in *Sodoms Ende*, he derives the right to deal with
them from the very fact that he has observed
them at a very close range, yet has proven himself immune against moral infection. True it is
that familiarity with the seamy side of life has
stripped him of many illusions, and surely it is a
matter for regret that because of his thorough
sophistication he is rather unsuccessful in the
dramatic presentment of innocence. Fritzchen in
Sodoms Ende is as insufferable a specimen of the
stage child as William Tell's precocious Walter.
Equally infelicitous is the portrayal of Klärchen
Fröhlich, the naïve victim of Willy Janikow. Much
more successfully drawn by contrast is Kitty, who
though for a while too close to the vortex of questionable gayeties, and engaged in some rather risky
flirtations, has remained sound at the core. Sudermann loves to operate with contrasting *milieus*.
In *Die Ehre* we had the *Vorder-* and the *Hinter-*
haus ; in *Sodoms Ende* the cramped snuggery of

Willy's impoverished, hard-working parents is held
up by the side of the splendid establishment of
Barczinowsky the speculator. This household is
a typical abode and rallying place of brazen up-
starts and reckless voluptuaries. Dr. Weisse, that
"incarnation of impertinence," says with a cynical
boast: "One is entirely *sans gêne* in these houses.
Here we talk like hostlers. That is the *fine fleur*
of social culture nowadays." That young Janikow is so easily infected by the pestilent moral
atmosphere which circulates in this den of arrant
luxury is perhaps proof sufficient that there is not
much to the man. And so it is difficult to understand why mature Frau Adah, her piquant niece
Kitty, and poor Klärchen Fröhlich fight for him
so madly. For a while things go swimmingly.
Willy is not really a bad man, for to be bad is
at least to have some character. He merely combines the traits of a thoroughgoing lazzarone and
an unqualified egoist. Nothing could be worse for
him than the adulation which greets him at every
turn, — from his poverty-stricken parents and his
unreasonably faithful friend Kramer at home, and
in the mansion of the rich stock gambler from the
seductive lady of the house. A stronger head than
his might be turned by so much frankincense and

myrrh. The impudent fellow indulges in liberties which loudly call for a flogging, but behold — all the world throws bouquets at him. A glaring instance is his declaration of his so-called love to Kitty. Is he, after all, but a harmless idler? Far from it. Sudermann holds that he who has been left at the wayside because he missed the train that was to speed him onward to his proper destination will, as a rule, bring destruction not only upon himself but on others also. And so Willy Janikow, that shining specimen of prurient genius who once expresses a passing curiosity to know "how an honest fellow feels," crushes the happiness of six human lives in the brief space of five theatrical acts, with about as much compunction as that with which a man swallows his half dozen oysters by way of prelude to dinner. Yet towards the end, after committing a twofold villainy against Klärchen and his loyal Kramer, he whines and whimpers, "Do me the last favor and kill me." Kramer, who has the tender sensibilities of Adam Bede and the "Manxman," cannot nerve himself to the deed. And so, as his hero cannot rise to the opportunity for a decent suicide, the playwright is compelled to invoke a most improbable, but fortunately fatal, hemorrhage.

We cannot help admiring the lifelike picture
of that class of society which dances — in Berlin
and elsewhere too — not, as the saying has it, on
the edge of a crater, but rather on the thin surface of a foul morass. Even more admirable is
the technical mastery shown in the construction.
The motivation of Kramer's threatening vengeance, the manner in which Willy Janikow's
mother discovers that Adah is her son's mistress, —
these and other incidents are unexcelled examples
of intelligent dramatic composition; and our grateful appreciation for these may make us indulgent
to the disgusting scene which presents Janikow
father and son both hopelessly the worse for
liquor, and to the somewhat theatrical soliloquy
which brings the piece to a close. *Sodoms Ende*
though realistic is not true to life; a satire is
always an exaggeration. Still, although the conditions of life which are presented in this play
do not impress one as actual or probable, they
do not seem impossible. The author has simply
culled the ingredients out of which the work is
distilled from a far greater area of observation
than is brought to view. He makes no effort to
palm it off as a piece of life. Even in this, the
most uncompromisingly realistic of his longer

plays, he does not attempt to reproduce the jargon of the every-day. The greater, then, the power of his craftsmanship, since he succeeds in spite of this in giving to his play such a considerable semblance of dramatic truth. I say truth advisedly, but do not mean the literal truth of life; of that even the most thoroughgoing realism is bound to fall short. The truth of a play consists in the playwright's power to make us accept illusions for facts.

Two years after *Sodoms Ende*, in 1893, *Heimat* (" Magda ") was performed for the first time, — a play in which the eclectic method of *Die Ehre* is again employed in preference to the greater naturalism of *Sodoms Ende*. The subject dealt with in " Magda " has been treated in a humorous vein by another modern writer, Ernst von Wolzogen, in his comedy *Die Kinder der Excellenz*. It in fact contains a strong serio-comic possibility. However, in " Magda " what humor there is, is episodic, incidental. The main drift is opposed to any form of levity, the satirical spirit held firmly in check by the serious purpose. "Magda" is the most brilliant defense of Sudermann's sociological thesis. A social conflict lies at the basis of the tragedy. The author resumes the subject already once

treated in *Die Ehre*, viewing it from a different
point under altered circumstances; carrying it,
in my estimation, to a more natural, or at any
rate to a more probable, conclusion. The olden
time, incarnate in the retired Lieutenant-Colonel
Schwartze, is in conflict with the new. Throne
and altar are struggling with new-bred ideals for
ethical supremacy. The form of the conflict may
seem antiquated in its poignancy, but thus the
clash in the tragedy is all the better prepared.
Now from this dramatic substructure arises the
private tragedy of a spirited individual revolting
against the caste in order to enforce a right to independent happiness. In the act of self-liberation
which necessitates the painful severing of sacred
ties, the play culminates. We have seen Robert
Heinecke in the throes of the same ordeal, but
he fought his battle by the side of a trusty and
powerful ally; moreover, the loathsome vulgarity
of his own people made the separation relatively
easy. It is different in *Heimat*. The hero this
time is a woman, — a woman who is put altogether
on her mettle. Do not think for a moment that
Sudermann's play deals with woman's "emancipation," as the word was understood twenty-five
years ago. For a modern writer of his way of

thinking the woman question has passed beyond
that theoretical stage. Since the overwhelming
majority of progressive-minded men has pronounced in favor of the admission of women to
higher studies and to the practice of arts and
professions, the ground is nearly cut out from
under the feet of the adversaries of the movement. Even for the German woman the realiza-
tion of her claims to equality has begun under
propitious auspices. It is quite in vain that
the little god to whom the male philistine has
erected an altar in his stomach still struggles
against the coming certainty, and questions with
an anxious sigh who is going to cook for him
after that.

Magda has left the paternal roof many years
ago in order to save herself from the crushing
tyranny of her father, a man who brings up his
family after the fashion of a petty sovereign,
instilling by rigid discipline, along with a reverence for his ideals, a thorough respect for the
great military phantoms of Pride and Honor. The
immediate cause of the rupture was Magda's refu-
sal to marry young Pastor Heffterdingk. She
goes to Berlin, first as companion to an old lady.
After a year she decides to go on the stage. The

news of this disgracing step so shocks the old officer that he has a paralytic stroke, from which he
never quite recovers. He is compelled to quit the
service, — a terrible blow for him. Thus Magda
is the cause of all his misfortunes. Meanwhile
what is her own fate? Utterly disowned by her
father, all alone in Berlin, where she struggles to
open a career for herself, the impulsive girl succumbs to the blandishments of a young barrister.
After he abandons her, she passes through the
vicissitudes of an artist's career to ultimate triumph. Now a famous prima donna, she has
returned under her stage name for a passing visit
to her native town, where she is to be the star in
a great music festival. The remembrance of her
father's despotism is still vivid within her and her
resentment unbroken. Nevertheless, she yields
to the persuasion of the unselfish Heffterdingk
and patches up a peace with her father, who, likewise through the pastor's efforts, though at first
terribly stirred, consents to receive her. Knowing that there can be no *entente* between her and
her people, that only a sense of piety still attracts
her to her home, Magda has no business to move
from the hotel to the paternal rooftree merely to
gratify her father's unreasonable whim. On this

point the old man really acts like a monomaniac.
If Magda should only stand her own ground
there would be no tragedy. Nobody knows this
so well as Sudermann, and that is just why she
must make the fatal concession. A mere removal
from hotel to house is made responsible for the
sequel! The problem of *Die Ehre* is here re-
stated, but this time it is viewed on the obverse
side, the spiritual reaction of the home people
under the contact with the " outsider " furnishing
the dramatic motive. That there must be a clash
is clear. The very contrast between Magda's free
mode of life and the narrow-gauge track along
which the family life is trailing, the contrast
between their straitened decorum and her somewhat stagy *sans gêne*, is bound to produce it.
Still, Magda may not stay long enough to make
serious trouble. But then there is Magda's past.
We understand that she is not a common adven-
turess, but shall we expect her father to draw
nice distinctions? Magda therefore sets the condition that her past life must not be stirred up by
any questions, and thus makes her entry into her
father's home with a stipulation which borders
dangerously on a *jeu de théâtre*. When I last
saw the play it was certainly either a symbolic

coincidence, or an intentional hint between acts, that after the drop of the curtain, immediately after Magda's injunction is laid down, the orchestra struck up the Lohengrin motive, "*Nie sollst du mich befragen!*" The question now is, How long will the unreasonable old gentleman, whom the very condition has put on the alert, live up to his promise and leave his daughter unmolested? In the third act he is the horrified earwitness of Magda's secret. Events now follow one another with sweeping force. The old soldier, beside himself with grief and shame, loses his head. It never occurs to him that if he would keep silence and allow Magda to go her way, he would be no worse off than he long had been. She has been a stranger to him for many years. He has not cared to know what has become of her. Even the mention of her name has been forbidden in his house. But as he has worn His Majesty's uniform, his sense of honor is always on the verge of an explosion. His only care is to scour the blot from his scutcheon. One hope only is left. Dr. Keller, Magda's seducer, who is at present a close political friend of Schwartze, a prominent member of a religious circle, and a conspicuous defender of the Good,

the True, and the Noble, must marry Magda;
then her family will all be rehabilitated. Keller
is a true representative of that detestable tiptoe
pharisaism known in Germany as *Strebertum*.
He is not troubled by the fact that Magda de-
spises him from the bottom of her heart as a
hypocrite who took advantage of her inexperi-
ence. He considers only his career, which would
be shattered by the scandal consequent upon
a duel with Schwartze. An understanding is
reached by his proposal of marriage. Through
the friendly mediation of Pastor Heffterdingk
Magda accepts the proposal. Keller then comes
out with conditions. Magda must leave the stage.
That he takes for granted with cavalier impu-
dence. But he demands further that she shall
permanently separate from their child. This is
the last straw. She orders him out of the house.
But the old colonel stands determined to compel
her to yield to the cruel demand. Now Magda,
realizing that she has again put her neck into
the iron collar of paternal authority from which
she had once freed herself, rises in revolt; her
child at least she will not sacrifice to such despotism. Her motive in this decisive fight for
liberty is not selfish. Magda's proud exclamation,

"I am myself and must not lose myself," must
not mislead us. We have seen her ready to
submit, to suffer abridgment of her personal
freedom, even to relinquish her brilliant career,
all for the sake of her old father, to whom she
feels that she owes reparation. But now her
maternal instincts rebel; and when she reflects
that such a heinous sacrifice is sanctioned by the
general code of morals, she tramples that code
into the dust. In her deep provocation she no
longer takes heed of the father. "*Und wenn er
nicht der einzige wäre—?*" she exclaims. To make
that marriage impossible she hints at liaisons
(probably fictitious) with other men. The father,
desperate, raises the pistol against the self-
declared courtesan, when a fatal stroke of apo-
plexy arrests his hand. Over his dead body
Magda steps again to her former freedom; not
without a share of punishment, for her conscience will never entirely acquit her of blame
for her father's anguish and death. Yet the way
in which Mrs. Patrick Campbell at the end of the
play kneels in the center of the stage, crying in
contrite tones, "My God! what have I done!"
is not true to the spirit of Magda. The heroine
of *Heimat* in this hour of agony must stand

forth — it is thus that Sarah Bernhardt interprets
the part — solitary, in lugubrious magnificence.

The opposite of Magda in conduct is Elizabeth, the central figure in the drama *Das Glück
im Winkel* ("Happiness in a Nook") (1896).
Elizabeth, named rightly (by Bulthaupt) "a Bac-
chante with a Madonna-soul," looks upon marriage as an asylum wherein the respectable may
seek refuge and safety when beset by temptation.
Else how could she ever have consented to marry
an elderly schoolmaster, unlovable in spite of his
kind heart and many sterling qualities? When
temptation returns, with the appearance in her
home of the man from whom she has fled, she
lacks the strength either to bear with quiet
endurance her self-inflicted martyrdom or vio-
lently to throw down her yoke like Magda. To
decide her fate requires the superior moral forti-
tude of another personality. Although what has
been said does not reflect against the nobility of
Elizabeth's character, it is somewhat difficult to
call her the heroine. Who then fills the principal
part? Can it be Röcknitz, the East Elbian ath-
lete, the "strong man" of the play, with his enormous chest expansion and dwarfed conscience?
He cheekily poses as the *Übermensch*, but is a

flat failure in the rôle. The real trouble with
him is that, far from being overman he is not
man enough, so that we wait in vain for an explanation between him and Elizabeth's husband,
Wiedemann. His grandiloquent boast that he
will not steal the latter's happiness, but boldly
take it, "face to face," etc., — when does he make
it good? I suspect that if Elizabeth, prevented
from self-destruction by her husband, resigns herself to the "happiness in a nook," her change of
heart is due to disappointment in Röcknitz — to
disillusionment — fully as much as to the con-
quering generosity of Wiedemann's love. In the
final explanation between husband and wife the
playwright has, to my feeling, gone too far in an
endeavor to win sympathy for the man's high-
mindedness. It transpires that Wiedemann had
proposed to Elizabeth, the homeless "poor relation" of the Röcknitzes, mainly from a phil-
anthropic motive; because he had suspected,
wrongly, that — she had been ruined by a faith-
less lover. Would it not be natural for Elizabeth
in her innocence and womanly dignity to resent
the suspicion? We look into the deep well of
Wiedemann's compassion with a mingled feeling of admiration, wonderment, and contempt; I

doubt if, on the whole, the revelation heightens
our liking for him. At any rate, the domestic
drama seems hardly concluded. Elizabeth has
learned to despise Röcknitz, whom she had
secretly loved all her life. That danger is moved
out of her path. But will she learn to love her
husband simply because by the author's fiat she
sees him in a new halo? It taxes our credulity
too much to believe in the possibility of such a
woman's happiness in her union with a plain and
elderly man who can have little to his credit in
her eyes beyond a good measure of kindliness
and a certain sort of latent moral heroism. And
is there in Elizabeth's temperament the possibility of complete renunciation? Why should we
assume that the old regret will trouble her no
more, of which she says: "And then come the
winter evenings when one stares into the lamp,
and the summer nights when the linden before
the house is in bloom. And you say to yourself,
Yonder somewhere lies the world and happiness
— but you sit here and knit stockings." Behind
Elizabeth's happiness looms a huge question mark.
Sudermann's own philosophy prompts our doubt
whether she will ever be happy with this husband. The two belong to different worlds.

Their love is a compromise love. We feel there is a sadly damaged spot in this marriage. It has been covered with a patch, but will the patch stick forever?

"Magda" is Sudermann's most successful play. *Das Glück im Winkel* stands far behind it in point of popularity. This may be because Elizabeth's character appeals less to the imagination of the star actress. But the play is very significant indeed; for its lesson is that the powerful individuality of Magda hews out its own fate, while Elizabeth's lesser personality has to be content with the lot assigned by the conventions. *Das Glück im Winkel* also marks a distinct turn in favor of the accepted morality and therefore a step in the ethics of the author. Similarly, it is the last treatment of one of his artistic problems, — the impact of two diverse spheres henceforth ceases to be of immediate interest to him.

In point of time between the two plays last named lies *Die Schmetterlingsschlacht* (" The Battle of the Butterflies ") (1895), a comedy, but by no means a pleasing one, and, in my opinion, without enduring worth. I dispense, therefore, with a detailed analysis. Still, as a piece of realistic *milieu* painting, this work surpasses all

previous efforts of Sudermann. The intimate life
of the lesser official class is completely exposed
to view, the contrast between its decorous penury
and the quite different tribulations of the manu-
facturing class being strikingly expressed through
the families Hergentheim and Winkelmann. Max
Winkelmann, the idealist, finds himself placed
between and above the two classes, somewhat as
Robert is in *Die Ehre*, since in respect to sentiment and conduct he stands on a higher level
than either. The plot of the play is entirely
subordinate to the characterization of the people
involved. The latter is exceedingly clever, especially in the case of the many-daughtered Widow
Hergentheim and the *commis voyageur* Kessler,
with his practical wisdom, gift o' gab, and non-
interfering conscience,— a classic type of one kind
of successful business man. The difficulty is that
the details in this comedy are obtrusive, and the
humor too much acidulated. The dramatist, again
over-anxious to point his moral, is too liberal with
his scorn, in consequence of which the work loses
much of that "high and excellent seriousness"
which should underlie every true satire.

Another point of resemblance with *Die Ehre* is
the outcome of *Die Schmetterlingsschlacht*. The

oldest of the Hergentheim girls, Elsa, a young
widow, has been carrying on a love intrigue
with Kessler. Rosi, the youngest sister, is the
innocent go-between. These clandestine relations are kept up even after Elsa has succeeded
in capturing Max Winkelmann, the son of the
rich manufacturer by whom the sisters are employed at decorative art work. The situation is
all but discovered by the prospective husband.
The Hergentheims, desperately loath to let go of
Max, on whom hangs their salvation from pinch-
ing poverty, resort to a most cruel measure. Max
is to be made to believe that not Elsa but her
youngest sister is Kessler's paramour. Rosi, who
is hardly more than a child, is forced by the
rest of the family to incriminate herself so as to
clear the reputation of her sister. In spite of her
piteous entreaties, the vicarious sacrifice is actually extorted from her, and that in the presence
of Max, whom she secretly loves. To me this is
the most revolting scene in any modern play.
However, the ruse is thwarted, and Max and Rosi
are allowed to make each other happy. This sat-
isfactory ending does not make a comedy, or
Die Ehre would have to be so classed. Certainly *Die Schmetterlingsschlacht* is a comedy

only in name. It is too grim in its humor, too
acrimonious in its mood, to dismiss the reader
with that serenity or satisfaction which is invariably derived from a true comedy. In spite of
the happy issue the play is unquestionably very
depressing.

The two plays that have just been discussed
conclude in a way the series of Sudermann's
social dramas, strictly so called.   Though social
questions are by no means banished from subsequent plays, they are henceforth not treated with
exclusive reference to a special case in hand, nor
even to our own time; rather they are considered
from a higher, more general human outlook, — *sub
specie aeterni.* This larger view, which in itself
need not be optimistic, is plainly indicated in
Morituri (1897), a collection of three one-act
plays without any organic interrelation, but dealing variously, as we shall see, with one and the
same psychologic theme.

The first of the series is named *Teja.* It is the
first work of Sudermann that does not mirror a
view of modern German life, for it throws on the
stage a segment of that Germanic antiquity with
which we have become fairly familiar through the
writings of Gustav Freytag, Felix Dahn, William

Morris, and others. The hero of the dramolet is
that last stern king of the Ostrogoths who, in the
lengthy, changeful struggle for existence forced
upon the Gothic tribes by Rome and Byzantium,
laid down his life, together with the lives of his
men.

Sudermann has brightened up the tragedy of
Teja's end and at the same time raised it to a
nobler pitch. This is the story as told in the play.
The Gothic host has dwindled down to a mere
handful of half-famished warriors who, intrenched
in their impregnable position, confidently await
the arrival of supplies. Every minute the pro-
vision ships are expected to heave in sight. At
this time of breathless suspense the Goths, obedient to an ancient law, have chosen a wife for
their king. The gloomy Teja has submitted with
resigned indifference to the will of his people.
This is his wedding day. Bishop Agila has just
finished the marriage sermon. But all through
the ceremony Teja's thoughts have wandered out
to the ships that are so eagerly watched for. For
them, and the fate of his people, for nothing else,
does he care. Almost immediately after the wedding he learns that treachery has delivered the
fleet into the hand of the enemy. There is no

hope left for the Goths to grasp at. They have only one alternative: they may slowly and ignobly perish of hunger among the rocky hollows of Vesuvius, or they may make a sortie and be slaughtered like cattle by the Hunnish butchers. Of course they choose the battle. The brave little band makes ready to seal with their blood the death warrant of their race. *Dulce est pro patria mori!* But they cannot go joyfully to their death, for they are a vagabond tribe; their only home is the camp, where dwell also their wives and children. These they are permitted to visit for the last time. But they are enjoined to take silent leave, for the king would not have even one of them unstrung by the tears and wailings of the women. The sequel shows that the woman-hating king does injustice to the Gothic maids and matrons. The first to convert him to a better opinion is his lovely Queen Bathilda. The whole pathos of Teja's life is compacted into the brief scene. In the eleventh hour the doomed man has learned for the first time to know happiness. He has laughed and frolicked with his bride till the moment when she must be told. She accepts the inevitable with naïve heroism; without any wild outburst of grief and despair she calmly kisses her husband's brow, thus consecrating him to death. Teja's eyes are opening more and more. In the last scene he says to the bishop: " I have insulted you this evening. Forgive me and accept my thanks, for now I also know why the Goth loves death." He seizes his sword, then to his men: " Well, are you ready? Is the farewell over? "

Theodemir: My lord, we have acted contrary to your orders. Which of our women guessed it and which one of us told it is hard to say. Enough, they all know it.

Teja: And so they set up a great lamentation?

Theodemir: My lord, they silently blessed us with the kiss of death.

Teja (startled, half to himself): They too! (*Aloud.*) Verily, we are a race of kings. Oh, the pity of our fate! Forward! (*He walks towards the background. The rest follow. The curtain falls amid the deafening cheers of the people greeting its king.*)

The theme of the masterly dramatic anecdote may be said to be the psychologic reaction of a character under the sudden certitude of death, and by this general problem *Teja* is closely inter-linked with the second, and, in my judgment, the best part not only of the collection but of Sudermann's dramatic work in its entirety.

It is entitled *Fritzchen*, deals with 'the present, and serves as a species of epilogue to *Die Ehre*. A boy lieutenant of the Prussian army, a good-natured, happy-go-lucky sort of a chap, has a liaison with a married woman. The wronged husband horsewhips him out of the house. Under the code of honor which obtains in the German army nothing can now avert a catastrophe. This code of honor, as everybody knows, does not shine for its logic. It generously condones many sins and peccadillos. The violation of the seventh commandment would not of itself hurt Fritzchen greatly in the eyes of his comrades. But the code never relents towards the officer who has suffered chastisement without taking bloody personal revenge. The still-remembered *Affaire Brüsewitz* and sundry like occurrences have served to enlighten the uninitiated as to the reason why the German officer in times of peace carries a keen-edged blade in the scabbard which we have heard clatter so smartly on the sidewalks of German cities. Now Fritzchen has been punished shamefully, and has not defended himself, because his saber was—not at hand. He may therefore thank

his lucky stars if the verdict of the regimental
Council of Honor to which the affair has been
referred is in favor of a duel; for an adverse decision would signify undying disgrace for Fritzchen.
He has come on a hurried farewell visit to his
home. Here, by prearrangement, he receives the
message: A duel has been decided on and must
be fought early on the morrow. Herr von Lanski
is a superior marksman and, as the challenged,
will lead off in the exchange of bullets. Fritzchen,
accordingly, is a doomed man. Moreover, it is
plainly hinted that he has made up his mind to
fall in the duel. With consummate skill and, as
one German critic well puts it, " unexampled dramatic laconism," the author now undertakes to
show how the pampered young *viveur*, who in
pursuance of his father's fatal advice has early
sown his full measure of wild oats against the
time of his manorial existence, turns sober in the
face of death. In his hour of gloom his manly
virtues come to the fore. As he hurriedly reviews
his squandered life there flits across his vision a
picture of that domestic happiness he would have
elected had he not allowed himself to be swerved
aside from his natural bent by the traditions of
his house. His home, his love, his prospects, they

are all in this sphere. But he is done with prospects, with love, with life itself. The brief tragedy
speeds from scene to scene, with a terrible incre-
mental force, till the climax is reached in the explanation between father and son; thence without
a halt to the most painful ordeal reserved for
Fritzchen, — the leave-taking from his invalid
mother, from whom the truth must be carefully
kept. The pathos of this parting is unspeakable,
the poor boy striving heroically to hide his heart-
ache under a boisterous feigned merriment; then
at last with tender deception leaving home, a merry
tune on his lips, as he goes straightway to his death.

Das Ewig-Männliche (" The Eternally-Masculine "), which is the last of the *Morituri* collection, is designated by the poet as a fantasy (*Spiel*).
And, to tell the truth, it has no more realism
than the fairy plays (*Märchendramen*) which came
into vogue about the time of its origin. In its
baroque costuming, this one-act comedy brings
to mind the preciosity of the age of Louis XIV,
immortally satirized by Molière. As, however,
Sudermann's satire is not directed against anybody in particular, the dramatis personæ are
labeled in a general way as " Queen," " Marshal
of the Court," " Ladies-in-waiting," " Marquis

in pale blue," "Marquis in pink," "Painter,"
etc., very much as in Goethe's *Die natürliche
Tochter.*

In contradistinction to all previous plays of
Sudermann, *Das Ewig-Männliche* is written in
verse, nay more, in rime. The example of the
author's ingenious friend, Ludwig Fulda, may
have had something to do with that. As in the
rimed comedies of Fulda, it should be added,
so here the language fairly scintillates with epigram and witticism. The play deals apparently,
like its two companion pieces, with the spiritual
state of a character unexpectedly confronted with
death. An artist who is painting the Queen's
portrait is made bold by the provoking coquetry
of the royal model. She listens, alarmed but
not displeased. The scene is interrupted by the
Marshal, who, himself in love with the Queen,
is ordered by her with great presence of mind to
cool his rival's ardor. The two men face each
other after the manner of Tasso and Antonio
in Goethe's *Torquato Tasso,* the part of greater
practical wisdom falling this time to the politic
artist. As a sensible man he realizes that he has
no better chances against the Marshal's sword
than the latter would have against his paint brush.

And so he proceeds cleverly to enlighten the love-blind warrior on the unworthiness of his idol. With the Marshal's consent and coöperation he improvises a little tragi-comedy; and when the Marshal, feigning death, gets a humiliating insight into the true inwardness of the adored woman, artist and courtier, arm in arm, go merrily into exile, leaving the handsome Jean, the Queen's impudent waiting-man, alone in the field as representative of the "Eternally-Masculine."

It has been shown that the three dramas do not constitute, in any dramaturgic sense, a miniature trilogy. The collective title is justified by a central idea; the difference hinges on the relations of men to ideals which vary with clime and time. In *Teja* we see the manifestation of a wholly ethnic consciousness, in *Fritzchen* the hero's conduct is inspired by sectional or specific class ethics. *Das Ewig-Männliche* is an almost cynical reversal of the *Fritzchen* tragedy, two men of force and value barely escaping the social folly of sacrificing life and limb to a vapid convention.

Sudermann's next play brought a surprise to his friends as well as to his adversaries. It was a biblical tragedy. It had become the fashion at that time, when literary art had practically passed out of extreme naturalism, to nose around for hidden symbolism in every new work of fiction. To seek any esoteric meaning in *Johannes* (1898), however, is to look for disappointment. Sudermann's hero is he of whom it is written in the third chapter of the Evangelist Matthew: "In those days came John the Baptist, preaching in the wilderness of Judea, and saying, Repent ye: for the kingdom of heaven is at hand. For this is he that was spoken of by the prophet Esaias, saying, The voice of one crying in the wilderness, Prepare ye the way of the Lord, make his paths straight. And the same John had his raiment of camel's hair, and a leathern girdle about his loins; and his meat was locusts and wild honey." In the New Testament the tragic ending of John the Baptist is subtly hinted rather than fully motived. Enough is left unexplained in the conduct of all concerned to have tempted more than one writer to venture an elaboration of the brief account. Sudermann's aim in treating the subject is to secure for the unfortunate preacher in the wilderness the fullest measure of our human sympathy. Let us see to what extent his purpose is attained. The forerunner of the gentle Nazarene is a hard-and-fast-bound Puritan, chained and paralyzed by his inflexible asceticism, without real understanding of the human heart, and therefore without compassion and charity. With a delicate psychologic instinct Sudermann explains the fall of the fanatical prophet through his spiritual awakening. John at first imagines the Messiah whom he heralds to be a kingly lord: "And wouldst thou know, woman, how he shall come?" proclaims the Baptist in act iii, scene x; "as king of the hosts, covered with an armor of gold, his sword uplifted over his head, he will come to save the Lord's own people. His enemies he will trample under the hoofs of his steed, but the young men of Israel will greet him exulting. Behold, O woman, thus shall he arrive." The Baptist's fundamental misconception of his mission works his destruction so soon as he, the fanatic of rabbinical lore, loses the absolute faith in himself; so soon as the Mightier One cometh after him, the latchet of whose shoe he is unworthy to unloose; so soon as he shudderingly opens his eyes and finds himself unequal to the work he has set out to do. John's fate is akin to Hamlet's: destiny has imposed a task upon him for which he is morally unprepared. The gradual conversion of such a character from mere virtuous rigor to real humanity

supplies a theme not only of dramatic but of
intense religious interest. Sudermann's play may
be called, by a figure of speech, a tract raised to the.
power of art, a comparison borne out, among other
ways, by the archaic solemnity of its language.
The story of John the Baptist as told in the Gos-
pels of Matthew, Mark, and Luke is greatly elab-
orated for the psychologic purpose of the play.
The following is an outline of the plot.

The Jewish people writhes in the fetters of a
twofold tyranny. Whatever of vitality is left to it
by the Roman oppressors is slowly sapped by the
Jews' own theocratic "Law," debased by bigotry
and priestcraft to a heart-and-soul-killing ritualism.
The mass of the people, instead of being quick-
ened at the fount of a living religion, are put off
with empty formulæ; thus they have turned into
a race of pessimists who, despairing of their power
of self-redemption, strain their longing eyes to
descry the Messiah of the prophetic message,
"whose fan is in his hand, and he will thoroughly
purge his floor, and will gather the wheat into his
garner; but the chaff he will burn with fire un-
quenchable" (Luke iii, 17). John himself is held
by a portion of the people to be the prophesied.
But his own consciousness tells him better: he is

but the harbinger of the Saviour. In this conviction the other-worldly man assumes provisionally
the part of a popular leader for which he is so ill
made. We find him at Jerusalem, inciting the
populace against the Tetrarch who, with brazen
adultery, has just flung a fatal insult at the pure
family morals of the Israelites. But at the very
start the hermit pines for his desert: "Am I set
as a lord over this people? Let the shepherd
drive his flock through thorns or flowers. I thirst
for solitude. I long for my rocks." Only by stern
constraint from within and without does he remain
at the head of the insurrection, a general without
a plan of campaign, a leader who knows not the
way. While he broods in this state of uncertainty
the word of Simon the Galilean strikes root in his
soul: "Higher than law and sacrifice is love," and
there is implanted in his soul the leaven of destruction; for the same message which paves for him
the way to a riper understanding unmans him
completely for his political enterprise: "Ye children of men, there is in your souls a roaring as of
many waters clear and troubled; I am to gather
all these into a mighty river, and I feel that I shall
drown therein." Even yet he remains unyieldingly
loyal to the old Messianic illusion, till he learns

with dismay from the lips of a beggar woman that his message holds no comfort for them that labor and are heavy laden, that these do not want his golden-panoplied Messiah.

Mesulemeth: Take thy message elsewhere. I will none of it.

John: What? You will none of the Messiah?

Mesulemeth: Not him, — not that one. For so many have come before clad in golden panoplies and have raised the sword so often that Israel bleeds like a sacrificial beast. Nor shall he be a king. When kings come, they come for the kings. To us poor none has ever come. Begone, O stranger! Thou strikest at my remnant of hope. Go! thou art a false prophet. Go! let me lie by the wayside.

The sting of this rebuke rankles in John's troubled soul. Just as he is making ready to lead the people against the sinful Tetrarch, the commandment that we should love our enemy, proclaimed in the land of Galilee by Jesus whom he baptized, comes to John and makes his hand drop the stone already raised against Herod. And this is the end of his leadership. In my opinion the whole plot gravitates toward this internal conflict, and not, as some have thought, about the temptation

of the Baptist by Salome. In the soul of John the
Baptist the same struggle goes on between the
old time and the new which we have already witnessed in Sudermann's social plays; but this time
the issue involves the fundamental history-shaping
attitude toward life, and the decision is therefore
wider in its bearing. The drama attains its purpose so soon as the power of the new spiritual
interpretation of life which we call Christianity
has conquered the theocratic world view in the
sentiment and will of the hero; then John may
calmly yield up his life for the new certainty: " I
hear all around me a mighty roaring, and the
blessed light well-nigh envelops me. . . . A throne
has descended from the heavens with pillars of
fire. And on it sits, clad in white raiment, the
Prince of Peace. And his sword is named ' Love,'
and 'Charity' is his battle cry." It is a fitter close
for this tragedy of a human soul than any other
Sudermann might have invented, that directly after
the beheading of John the Baptist loud, exultant
hosannas announce the entry of the Nazarene
into Jerusalem.

With all his force and skill and depth of conviction Sudermann does not fully attain his immediate object of compelling a fellow-feeling for

Johannes on the part of the beholder, and thus he misses, in part at least, the object of all tragedy, which is to awaken pity and fear. Only when, through the unraveling of the human fate to which we are made privy, we are made to beat our breasts, and when the Mahavákya, the "great word" of the Vedas: *Tat tvám asi* ("This is thou"), rises spontaneously to our lips, only then may the poet glory in having set free those potent emotions. We of the twentieth century have too little in common with a man who in his far-off desert has weaned himself from all passion and frailty, whose nature is steeped in a frigid, forbidding virtue, and whose personal purity is but the lusterless reflection of a gloomy, loveless self-righteousness. Herodias speaks from our own hearts when she hurls her rebuke against the unapproachable saint: "He who would presume to be a judge over men must have a share in their lives and be human with his fellows. But thou seemest to dwell in regions so far away that even the throbbing of the human heart seems to thee a folly. . . . Thou hast timidly shrunk from every sin, retiring like a coward into the solitude, and now crawlest forth to call others guilty. Maybe the fiery winds of the desert have taught thee to hate; but what

knowest thou of those who live and die for the
sake of their love?"

For yet another reason John the Baptist is unfit
to be the hero of a tragedy. In the crisis of his
dramatic development, when at last the true
humanity fires his whole being, he cannot lead
mankind forward and up to better, higher things,
for his spiritual energy does not become kinetic,
he is only a passive, uncreative character.

The most imposing figure in the play is the
woman Herodias. Like Lady Macbeth, she is an
incarnation of ruthless, violent ambition. She has
lent a willing ear to the wiles of Herod, not in
order to earn by fawning and begging a daily
offering of caresses, not for the gratification of
her feminine vanity, but in order to have absolute
power over him: to be not his mistress but his
master. John shall be for Herodias the ardently
desired tool of her political aggrandizement. To
purchase so rare an instrument even the youthful
charms of her daughter seem not too high a price
to her. It is seen at this point that Sudermann,
like others before him, seeks to motive the part of
Herodias in the fate of John. In this he is successful, but far less successful is he in his interpretation
of Salome's ready acquiescence in her mother's

design. To the adolescent Salome John the Baptist is primarily a male, no more, no less. In her veins the wayward blood of her race runs riot. Her premature, unwholesome sensuality is directed upon the shaggy apostle, not despite but because of his singularity. Thus she appears tainted with a pathologic perversity and seems to belong not properly to the world of the New Testament, but rather to the morbid vaporings of an August Strindberg, Marcel Prévost, or Catulle Mendès. Quite as diseased as her infatuation for the wild man from Judea is her revulsion against him when he scorns her, her truculent revenge, and her savage triumph over the victim's severed head.

The Herod of the play scarcely deserves mention: a slinking, venal degenerate; the fox of the Scriptures (Luke xiii, 31–32), not sly enough to be more than a cringing pander to the insolent Roman, and a callow puppet in the hands of his concubine.

Despite the freedom with which the story of the Baptist as told by the Evangelists is treated, Sudermann's *Johannes* is in form and substance a biblical play; hence it is a natural desire to draw from it some inference as to the poet's relation to the Christian faith.

In this regard too, as in all others, Sudermann is found to be a modern man. The time is happily past in Germany when to rail or sneer at every positive religious belief was to give evidence of polish and intellectual distinction. On the other hand, too, the divines and laymen of every creed have gradually adopted a more respectful and tolerant tone toward their honest adversaries. The disposition of the modern German who lays claim to real culture—that is to say, not education of the mind alone, but also of the sensibilities—is to bow in reverence before that genuine piety in which the orthodox Christian and Jew, the liberal, the dissenter, and the earnest agnostic have a common meeting ground. And that is, at the last, the reiigion of St. John the Baptist. It consists in the same genuine godliness which was upheld in the sixteenth century by honest, simple-hearted Hans Sachs, when during the high tide of religious strife he naïvely gave it as his opinion that "the ancient test of a Christian is charity, and not the eating of flesh, for cats and dogs can do that too."

Sudermann's next play, *Die drei Reiherfedern* (" The Three Heron-Plumes") (1898) differs curiously from all its predecessors. The author calls

it "a dramatic poem"; in reality it belongs to the
class of the fairy play and may be grouped with
Hauptmann's *Die versunkene Glocke* and Fulda's
Der Talisman, albeit the *Märchen* in *Die drei
Reiherfedern* is constructed by Sudermann's own
fancy, unaided by any relationship to folklore or
mythology, and must therefore depend upon its
intrinsic fascination for whatever interest it may
enlist. Once before, in *Das Ewig-Männliche*,
Sudermann strayed into the world of poetic caprice. The dramatic plot in " The Three Heron-
Plumes" is the mere vehicle of an allegory, and
the technical treatment is in frank contravention
of the naturalistic prescript. Here, as in " The
Eternally-Masculine," we find types and not real
individuals, if we except at most Prince Witte's
fiercely faithful retainer, the rough, colossal Hans
Lorbass, *baumlang und ungeschlacht*, as he is described in the play. The hero himself lacks dramatic personality; he is but the shadowy symbol of
the restless, insatiable cravings of an idealist with
those same emotional aspirations which so many
German poets have felt tempted to fathom. " The
tireless child of Desire" he calls himself, and he
is, indeed, a literary cousin of Faust, Don Juan,
and Master Heinrich the bell-founder.

It is his tragical destiny to spend his life in a
forlorn chase after the happiness which all the
time he holds unwittingly in his grasp. Sent on
an adventurous expedition by the graveyard witch
(*Begräbnisfrau*), a character that calls to mind
Hauptmann's Granny Wittichen, Prince Witte
takes from a sacred white heron three feathers
which possess magic power. If he throws the
first of them into the flames, Witte will behold
the dim likeness of his ideal woman, the blessing
of whose love is to illumine his existence. When
the second feather is burnt that woman shall appear before him, walking in her sleep. But when
the third feather falls to ashes that embodi-
ment of his ideal love must die. Prince Witte,
just returned, puts the first feather to the test; the
vague outline of a gigantic woman appears on the
horizon and slowly vanishes into the air. Her
features Witte has not been able to see. If ever
he meets her, how shall he recognize her? Soon
he comes to the court of the beautiful widowed
queen of Samland, who, for the sake of her people,
has promised to marry him who shall overcome
all other suitors. She falls in love with Witte
even before he enters the lists to win her, but he
is felled to the ground by the Duke Widwolf, his

bastard brother, the same who drove him from his inherited dukedom of Gotland, and who now claims the hand of the queen as his right. However, Lorbass, with the queen's warriors, sets upon the insolent usurper, putting him and all his fighting men to flight. The queen, contrary to her sworn promise, marries Prince Witte, who is to rule over the land until his little stepson shall have come of age. But to Witte's hazy longings after the unknown love and his disgust with the commonplace are superadded the pangs of conscience because of his own and his consort's perjury. Under the weight of remorse his activities slacken, and gradually his better nature falls into a torpor. He neglects his royal office, surrenders himself to wild revelries, and allows the royal sword to grow rusty. Yet his soul continues to yearn for its ideal. While in this torn state of mind he burns the second plume in the dead of night. To his amazement his own wife appears, walking with eyes closed in sleep. On Witte in his blindness the coincidence makes no impression. He bitterly upbraids the queen, whom he suspects of spying on his nightly carousals, and draws away from her farther than ever. Sinking deeper and deeper in his sloth, he at last refuses

to head his people against Widwolf, who has come
to wreak his vengeance. As a last heroic remedy
against the lethargic apathy of the king the rude
giant Lorbass, — in this play, with a possible
significance, the morals of the overman are dele-
gated to a subsidiary character, — having read
the king's mind, determines to kill the young heir
apparent. With the prince out of the way, so
he reasons, the king will rise to his office, for
he will then have to fight for his own, not for a
"borrowed" kingdom! But even as Hauptmann's
Poor Heinrich gains a saving triumph over his
selfishness, so King Witte is roused at last from
his culpable indolence, not through a crime but
through his better nature. The grim Hans Lorbass, having softened at the critical moment,
returns with the boy. At this sight the king,
who has been crazed by self-accusations, recovers
himself. With zeal he assumes his royal task in
the nick of time. His valiant arm soon lays low
the enemy who storm the palace. The kingdom
is safe. And Witte? *Errette mich vom Alltag!*
(" Deliver me from the everyday!") With this
exclamation he demands the freedom of which he
has dreamed for years. Together with his faithful
Lorbass he leaves his "purloined" grandeur and

resumes the aimless pursuit of his hazy ideal.
After fifteen years spent in a vagabondage full of
hardship and disappointment, the aging, thoroughly disillusioned man finds himself again near
the hut of the graveyard hag, broken in spirit
and weary of life. His eyes have begun to open
to the fact that he threw away his happiness
when he should have held it fast. He grasps the
whole truth when the queen appears on the scene,
full of love and forgiveness. Now when his course
is nearly run he realizes that he has misspent his
life in the childish pursuit of a bubble. In order
at last to cast off the spell which he now regards
as the source of his failure, he throws the third
feather into the fire. As the flames blaze over
the mystic plume the queen sinks to the ground
dying. And with the cry *"Du warst's!"* Witte
breaks down over her body.

We do not fail to notice a certain parallel
between this play and the tragedy of John the
Baptist. Both men are led into destruction by a
false idealism. As John still looks expectantly
for the coming of the gold-clad Messiah when all
the while Christ in his spiritual glory is walking
on earth, so Prince Witte consumes himself in the
idle search after that which he already possesses, —

the magnanimous love of a perfect woman. " The
Three Heron-Plumes" is a work of great poetic
merit. And yet, despite its many beauties, it
is, on the whole, Sudermann's least successful
work, if we except his latest, *Der Sturmgeselle
Sokrates*, compared to which everything else
he has ever written is a masterpiece. Versatile
though he is to an unusual degree, his genius is
hardly adapted to romance and fairy tale. Sudermann is too much a man of the modern world,
too much a Northerner and a Prussian. As he,
possibly more than any other writer of the new
generation, draws intellectual breath from the
atmosphere of criticism which pervades our times,
he is at his best when dealing with those questions which have the greatest moral actuality, and
with which it is consequently wholly legitimate
and proper that the modern play and the modern
novel should mostly concern themselves.

The plays which still remain for discussion
afford Sudermann that opportunity. The first
bears the symbolic name *Johannisfeuer* (" St.
John's Fire") (1900). The meaning of the symbolism in the play is made clear by the following declamatory outpouring of the leading male
character. " In every one of us there smolders

a spark of heathenism. This has outlasted the
thousands of years since the old Germanic times.
Once a year it bursts into a high flame and
then it is called *Johannisfeuer*. Once a year
there comes a night of liberty. Yes, yes, a night
of liberty. Then the witches ride with mock-
ing laughter up the Brocken on their broomsticks, the same broomsticks with which at other
times their witchcraft is cudgeled out of them.
Then the Wild Chase passes over the forest;
then awaken in our hearts the wild desires
which life has not fulfilled and which, mark me
well, it could not fulfill. For no matter what be
the name of the law that for the time happens
to rule in the world, — in order that the *one*
wish may be realized by whose grace we can
spin out our existence, a thousand other wishes
must perish miserably: some, possibly, because
they were forever unattainable, others — well,
others because we have allowed them to flit away
like wild birds over which our hand was too slow
in closing. ... Be this as it may, once a year
comes the night when we are free, and do you
know what it is that blazes yonder? do you know?
It is the phantoms of our deadened desires; it is
the red plumage of the birds of paradise which

perhaps we might have cherished all our life long, and which have taken wing from us; it is the old chaos; it is the heathenism within us. And be we never so happy in the sunshine and according to law, — this is St. John's Eve. To its old heathen fires I pledge my glass; this night may they blaze high and higher.[1] — Will no one touch glasses with me?" (act iii, scene iii). We can well understand why, after this somewhat extravagant tirade of Georg von Hartwig, an embarrassing silence ensues round the board of Squire Vogelreuter. This is broken at last by the heroine, Marikke, who with trembling hand touches her glass to Georg's as she says " I will," and looks him firmly in the eye.

In two breasts the fire of St. John breaks out in this play, which ends tragically enough. Though its pages flow not with blood, yet two lives — herein lies the tragedy — are consumed as a sacrifice savory in the nostrils of that ruling power, the law, — the morals which "happen for the time to rule the world."

Ethically considered, the play may or may not mark a step in the direction of the author's

[1] The pun on *Hoch*, the customary ending of a German toast, is lost in the Englishing.

philosophic reconciliation with that power. That would depend on the interpretation of the outcome. Dramatically considered, it certainly gives no proof of advance. The play suffers from the fact that Sudermann has this time yielded too freely to his strong liking for effects. Certain melodramatic elements, called in merely for decorative purposes, have unfortunately sneaked into the inner mechanism of "St. John's Fire." These ornamental features include more than the *double entendre* in the name of the play, the importation of symbolical illustrations, and notably the factitious interspersion of the dialogue with bits from the author's commentary on his own work, such as we hear in *Die Ehre* from Count Trast, and in *Sodoms Ende* from Dr. Weisse and Professor Riemann, or in *Die Schmetterlingsschlacht* from the invaluable Kessler.

With these, on the whole, we need have no quarrel in a dramatist who does not pose as a naturalist and probably has no special aptitude in that direction. The ideal drama, of course, should be self-explanatory. But even greater playwrights than Sudermann — and that is saying not a little — have fallen back on the same devices as he. Within æsthetic limits a writer is privileged to introduce *Stimmungsmittel*, that is to superinduce artificially the effect of his work. At most we may raise an objection against his almost insulting plainness in the explanation of things that are sufficiently clear in themselves. Georg's toast certainly verges dangerously on the *haec fabula docet*. Besides, the parallelism between fact and symbol need not be accentuated so much throughout the drama. The story gains nothing in probability from the circumstance that the outbreak of Georg's and Marikke's mutal infatuation is made simultaneous with the bonfires of St. John's Eve. It is sufficiently dramatic in its true inwardness. The picture could have well dispensed with the excessive ornament of its symbolic frame. Let that pass. But Sudermann, as was said above, goes to obnoxious lengths in touching up the sober tragedy of this play with melodramatic effects. He ransacks the Thespian van of itinerant barn-stormers, where he discovers his female tramp, the *Weszkalnene*. He stirs up the lumber room of Italian opera and culls a meaning reference to the fatal Mancheneel-tree of Meyerbeer's *L'Africaine*. He even plants an exotic tree of his own, the *Liriodendron Tulipifera* of the second act, and he shows half a mind to turn its blossoms to tragic account; but remembering, it may be, that he himself has done his share towards destroying the credit of fate-bringing vegetables and similar stage properties, he happily desists from the purpose. For after the flowering twig is dropped and the tarred barrels are burnt out, real forces, potent and plausible, are seen to be responsible for the sequel.

First of all is the moral organization of the two central figures, their temperament, by which their fall and fate are predetermined. Here it is heredity that reveals itself as nowhere else in Sudermann's plays. Georg comes of a masterful race, hence he belongs to the "*Herrenmenschen*," albeit he is a weak specimen of this strong modern genus. Marikke, on the other hand, being the daughter of a drunken, thievish beggar woman, it follows, according to Sudermann's theory of the transmission of traits, that she must steal. But whereas the old Lithuanian wretch, her mother, is principally out for food and underclothing, the daughter — what a singular form of kleptomania! — cannot resist an impulse to steal her portion of happiness. *Meine Mutter stiehlt. Ich stehle auch!* It is with these words that she throws herself away. The sweet,

housewifely girl whom they all call *Heimchen*
("the cricket on the hearth"), and who, though a
poor foundling, has been tenderly reared by the
Vogelreuters, is driven to her ruin by a mingled
feeling of love, sensual impulse, generosity, and
— this is the element incongruous with the general view of her character — reckless, fatalistic
insouciance. The outlines of these two principal
characters as sketched in by the author are
plainly discernible. Unfortunately the figures do
not fit themselves to the contours. Georg has
no true kinship with the "Master Folk." At bottom he is a boastful, vacillating, and selfish philistine. This, his real nature, is not disclosed to
those about him, nor to himself, — if at least the
playwright saw through him! But we have the
feeling that such is not the case, hence our own
puzzled state. It must be admitted that just as
there are inscrutable characters in life, so certain
dramatic characters of great depth, like Hamlet,
Faust, Wallenstein, baffle offhand interpretation.
As a rule, however, the character that fails to body
forth unquestionably the author's real conception
is to be regarded as a dramatic miscarriage.

Beside the not altogether adequate account-
ing for the tragedy through the driving force of

congenital character, there is put in commission
an auxiliary course of events which leads the prin-
cipals straight to the trapdoor of destiny. Georg
von Hartwig is, like Marikke, a *Notstandskind*
laid under an oppressive debt of gratitude. After
his father's suicide Georg has been educated
through the generosity of his uncle Vogelreuter.
While yet a schoolboy he has fallen in love with
Marikke. She, however, has not realized the depth
of his affection for her, and he has imagined
himself scorned. The play opens four days prior
to the marriage of Georg to Trude Vogelreuter,
a sweet, clinging damosel with a heartful of love
and a thimbleful of brains. The match, as far
as Georg is concerned, is to be conceived partly
as a requital of past benefits received from his
uncle, and partly as a *mariage de défi*, to spite the
Heimchen. The dramatic argumentation of both
points, however, is unsupported by cogent evidence. We only learn that in those past days
Marikke has repelled with natural pride the
demonstrations of the youngster's callow affection. So, for instance, one day when he followed
her into the cellar she managed to lock the
ardent lover in for a whole night, with the hope,
possibly, of reducing his spirits to the temperature

and harmlessness of the milk stored there. After that the facile psychologist considered his fate as sealed. "And since things had come to such a pass that I could not get you," he explains in act iii, "I afterward took Trude." Then this brilliant reader of the feminine mind adds, wonderingly, "Have you never realized that this was the way things hung together?" At the critical moment, when the Heimchen's repressed temperament is set aflame by the reappearance of Georg, two events ripen the catastrophe: the discovery of Georg's early love for her through some boyish poetry that turns up in an old drawer; and the arrival of her mother, the dissolute Weszkalnene, by which Marikke is thrown into a state of the utmost self-depreciation.

Marikke, then, "steals" her bit of happiness, but magnanimously rejects Georg's half-hearted offer to break off the marriage with Trude. It is at this point that the internal dramatic workings seem leavened with the ethical policy of the author, in that Georg and Marikke subordinate their love to a tender regard for their responsibilities to the family. The play ends with Georg and Trude going to the altar as if nothing had happened, while Marikke looks after them, her handkerchief between her teeth to stifle the out-cry of her anguish. If there is any "lesson" in this bourgeois ending, it seems to the superficial observer as though it can hardly be other than approbation, for once, of social authority, and a rebuff for insubordination of the individual. A play with such a message would seem to show the author of "Magda" and "Honor" in the attitude either of a convert or of a renegade. Before we jump to such a rash conclusion, however, it is well to pause before two other possibilities. May it not be that the ending of the play is either a grim satire or an uninterpreted illustration of reality? The last is certainly the least probable, for we have seen heretofore that Sudermann is not in the habit of keeping back his opinion. *Johannisfeuer* is weaker than it would be if this large question were not left open. Yet even now, if we look in some detail at the remainder of Sudermann's recent works, they may help to disclose the real meaning of this one.

The moral tone of the tragedy *Es lebe das Leben* ("The Joy of Living") (1902) argues conclusively against a radical change of front in the current ethical phase of Sudermann's literary activity.

Its burden is the exaltation of a life intense
and personal over the drag of an existence con-
ducted by rule of thumb in the interest and for
the convenience of the species. Yet Sudermann
indorses very positively the just claims of society
upon the individual. There is abundant happiness to be found beyond the pale of the law, but
the purchase price is so high, fortunately, as to
frighten off all but a few.

For the first time Sudermann in " The Joy of
Living " takes us into German high life. Count
Kellinghausen, prominent member of the conservative party, has laid down his electoral mandate
and used all his influence for the election of his
friend, Baron Richard von Völkerlingk. The sacrifice of his own political preferment has been
made at the prompting of his wife, Beate, who
is the Egeria of the party, and at whose table,
"*entre poire et fromage*," the fate of many a parliamentary bill has been sealed. She has per-
suaded Count Michael of his own unfitness for
parliamentary life, and has convinced him that
the highest interest of the party demands that he
decline his reëlection in favor of his more brilliant
friend. Under her wise direction Richard von
Völkerlingk has fully developed his rare political

powers. His son Norbert, under the same influence, has matured into an earnest sociological
thinker. Norbert loves Countess Beate better
than his own mother and is tacitly accepted as
the prospective husband of her daughter Ellen.
The love of the young people only supplies the
rather hackneyed underplot. The pivotal figures
of the main plot are Richard von Völkerlingk
and Beate von Kellinghausen. They have known
each other for fifteen years. From the start
they have been intimate friends, soon becoming
lovers. To the quiet little woman that Beate
used to be, Richard's superior mind has unlocked
the wealth of a new and larger life; under his
guidance she has grown to be a woman of strength
and purpose, able to repay in kind by becoming
a wise counselor to Richard, and forming the
character of his boy. Their culpable relations
have mellowed after a short time into a fraternal
affection, a soul companionship from which both
draw the courage to continue their lives. Beate's
ambition dreams of a great future for Richard,
and because she cannot bear to see his talents
lying fallow, she creates the opportunity for him
to exercise them. Richard's conscience naturally
recoils from so great an indebtedness to the man

whom he has betrayed. But he has yielded to
Beate's persuasion and has just been returned
to Parliament. In the impending debate on the
divorce question he is to raise his voice as the chief
spokesman of his party in defense of the sacredness and indissolubility of marriage. His sense
of honor is greatly disturbed at this; he is not
a man who can make shift with the assumption
that people will be guided by his public words,
not by his secret actions. He feels that whatever
he says in his political capacity should be uttered
without an inward contradiction. Withal he is
heart and soul in his task. The suggestion of
a tragical ending arises spontaneously. Richard
may appear as the champion of morals but once.
By a great speech he may decide the victory of
the cause. Then in the midst of his triumph he
may certify to its truthfulness by his death. To
a fecund inventor of plots like Sudermann this
single thread seemed too slender, so it is reën-
forced by a political intrigue and at the same time
by the frustration of Richard's suicide through the
ingenious self-sacrifice of Beate. For her action,
of course, the author must furnish a strong motive,
and thus Beate becomes from this point on the
real heroine of the play.

Count Michael is accidentally informed of what he firmly believes to be a groundless defamation of his house, and decides to punish the slanderer. He has perfect confidence in his wife and his friend, but lest some triviality be puffed up into a serious accusation against them, he wants to know if they have any recollection of any detail in their mutual relations which might lend the slightest color of truth to the charge of undue intimacy. Finally he asks for Richard's word of honor that nothing need be feared in the way of evidence. Thus very unexpectedly the climax is brought on. Richard starts to "perjure himself like a gentleman," but Beate prevents. "Now he will give you his word of honor and then he will go home and put a bullet through his head." At this moment she stakes, nay more than that, she surrenders her all in order that Richard may again be at one with himself, once the great lie is ousted from his life. And she explains to her husband in this confession scene why she has lived the lie at his side for half a lifetime. Suppose she had obtained her freedom, and Richard his too, would she not have completed the wrecking of his life if she had stuck to him as the relic of a past scandal? Count Michael von Kellinghausen, after this crushing exposure, is not in a position to exact the customary satisfaction; the playwright has crossed his purpose, for reason. Before Michael entered upon the prosecution of the slanderer he had to pledge his word to his political friends that the party should be carefully protected against the taint of scandal. Accordingly a settlement between him and Richard in conformity with the ordinary rules of the code of honor is practically impossible. By a dramatic *coup de force* Völkerlingk junior much earlier in the play has unwittingly pronounced sentence of death on his father. Being the author of a pamphlet on the question of dueling which evinced a liberal tendency quite at variance with the views of his social circle, he was upholding the thesis of his pamphlet against Count Michael and Baron Richard, who both maintained, from different positions, that in certain cases, when irreparable offense has been given, gentlemen must appeal their dispute to the decision of arms. Norbert expressed the opinion that the offender, if he be a man of honor and willing to make atonement, would do best to act as his own judge.

The two men now fall back on Norbert's verdict. Richard takes a reprieve of forty-eight hours to arrange his affairs in a way to leave no clew to the motive of his suicide.

The dramatic problem in the last two acts is to bring the affair to a conclusion in such a manner that Beate's great sacrifice shall not have been in vain. The tremendous effect of Völkerlingk's speech on the sanctity of marriage has opened before him the possibilities of a career than which no living man has achieved a more splendid; a career which nothing but a scandal can blast. He is universally regarded as the coming man. Beate realizes that Richard has paid, with his resolution to die, for the right to speak as he has on that subject, and she also knows that by his first great success life has been endeared to him, and he is full of a secret avidity to live. Her mind is made up to save him. Her own life, in constant jeopardy on account of heart disease, seems to her a more suitable sacrifice. If she dies, so Beate calculates, Völkerlingk is bound to live in order to save her reputation and the happiness of the young couple. She induces her husband to invite Richard to a gentlemen's gathering so as to nip in the bud any rumors of a scandal. Then she secures Richard's promise to attend.

In the fifth act, which is marred by some glaring theatricalities, Count Kellinghausen's breakfast party is represented. Beate, who is the only woman present, proposes a somewhat exorbitant toast to the joy of living. With the words *"Es lebe das Leben!"* she drains a poisoned cup. A letter left behind explains to her husband the purpose of her death. Michael and Richard now realize that their covenant is void. Richard may—nay, must—live, and Michael offers no opposition to the union of Ellen and Norbert. And yet it cannot be asserted that the end of Beate's self-destroying act is wholly attained. "And you understand"—these are the closing words of Richard to Michael—"that I must live, though I do not care to—must live—because I am dead. Farewell."

Nearly all the characters in "The Joy of Living" are conventionalized, a fact which explains in a great measure the friendly acceptance of the play in England and the United States, where the public shows such conservative aversion to the admission of strangers into stage land. The heroine, however, forms a notable exception.

The Countess Beate, who has become a favorite star part for traveling tragediennes, is not the sole

specimen of her kind. On the contrary, she belongs to a numerous sisterhood. Nevertheless
she has a personal note which separates her from
the magnanimous adventuresses of French drama,
and from all the heroines of Ibsen, and Pinero,
and Sudermann himself. She is distinguished
by a consuming "will to live," in gratifying
which she is not hampered, as is her lover, by any
moral scruples. In the words of Thomas Carlyle,
she conquers remorse by avoiding it. This is not
to say that she is without a moral conscience;
rather she has one all her own. By the code of
morals which as social and political beings we
confess, the Countess Beate von Kellinghausen
stands condemned, and not even by her many good
deeds can she be recommended to mercy. Yet
inasmuch as it is our laudable custom to relax the
check upon our generous impulses when viewing
conduct not in life but on the stage, the Rhada-
manthine judgment on the sinning Beate softens
greatly before the pleadings of her palliating traits.
She is guilty beyond a doubt, and her guilt is
largely aggravated by her remorseless, jubilant
spirit. In this she is of the Nietzschean mold,
and resembles Magda pointing out with shocking
pride the connection between her trespasses and

her vital sense of freedom. Beate, indeed, cherishes a passionate love of life in its rich and variegated fullness. But she loves it not only for what it holds for herself: she is even ready to fling her own share away in order to secure for her best beloved a greater participation in the joy of living. She has been so far a seeker after happiness for others that when we examine the portion that she has kept for herself it will be found to consist in the self-imposed martyrdom of love. And so, with the footlights marking off a safe distance between Beate and ourselves, since it seems that human compassion must keep a distance, " her sins which are many are forgiven, for she loved much." " The Joy of Living" has been treated here at greater length than many of Sudermann's plays. The reason was partly the success that play has experienced on the English as well as on the German stage, and partly the fact of its being an important document in Sudermann's ethics.

It confirms, in a sense, the moral individualism observed throughout his career as a writer. At the same time it shows a fair acquiescence in the restraint put upon individual conduct by the common agreement of society. However elating Beate's joy of living, the wages of her sin, after all, is death. The two sentiments, as has been already mentioned, are not necessarily contradictory. Sudermann, to put it plainly, was from the beginning, and has remained to this day, a believer in the exception by which the rule is proved.

Whenever a contemporary writer who has shown the strength requisite to divide public opinion as to his true importance passes through the temporary eclipse of a real failure, a self-constituted coroner's jury of his enemies will inevitably pronounce him dead from exhaustion. They knew all the while, it goes without saying, that he was growing decrepit; that his triumphs were only the galvanic signs of life produced by ingenious self-advertisement; they had predicted that sooner or later the bottom would be knocked out of the workbox from which came all the flimflam of his cheap effects. They had looked forward with alacrity to the future which would bear out their forecast that the reputation of the writer in question was wholly evanescent.

In Germany more than in any other country great importance is attached to questions of literature; consequently a writer like Sudermann cannot wonder at having a multitude of critics.

Without invoking the apologetic *Quandoque bonus dormitat Homerus*, it may be said in a spirit of justice that no attitude on the part of a critic can be more petty and unfair towards an earnestly striving artist than the malignant appraisal of his worth on the basis of the least creditable of his performances. Hermann Sudermann has been signally unsuccessful with his last play, the comedy *Der Sturmgeselle Sokrates* (1903). That even his stanchest adherents will have to admit. And the failure was not confined to a single feature of the play; the entire work in regard to structure, form, and substance, plot, language, and characters is past saving. Worst of all, the spirit in which it is written is to be unequivocally condemned. *Der Sturmgeselle Sokrates* is a libelous caricature on the lofty political idealism that inspired the so-called *Völkerfrühling*, the outbreak of the German love of liberty in the year 1848. The story of the play not really being worth the telling, it is sufficient to touch upon its main points. In a small East Prussian city, by which is doubtless meant Tilsit, there exists in the middle of the seventies a club called *Die Sturmgesellen*, "the Fellow Stormers." It is composed of five or six oldtime chums, nearly all eccentric and wrong-headed

old codgers, who meet once a week in a dingy
public house and pass the evening with beer,
tobacco, and political drivel. They are the innoc-
uous remnant of a secret society founded in the
early fifties, soon after the suppression of the
revolution, one of the many which in the period
of reaction kept alive clandestinely the democratic
hopes. The solemn absurdities of this obsolete
conspiracy are kept up with ludicrous punctilious-
ness. The puerility of the old Fellow Stormers is
not without its touch of pathos. While they still
throw around at a lively rate their high-sounding
balderdash about liberty, equality, and fraternity,
their political creed has gone out of date and lost
its meaning, and they appear to be blind to the
fact that a new era has realized many of their
ancient dreams. So far so good. The ludicrous
yet touching loyalty to the moribund idols of
one's generous youth might have proved a fruitful theme for a serio- or even a tragi-comic play.
And such an one was probably in the author's
mind. Unfortunately Sudermann committed a
double error. In the first place, he took the
tempora mutantur altogether for granted and
emphasized unduly the *et nos mutamur* in his
characterization of the *Sturmgesellen*, by making

them out, with a single exception, as a set of thorough-paced idiots and hypocrites. Their conduct is for the most part utterly inconsistent with their professed high principles, besides being discreditable to their intellects. One of them is a sordid timeserver; another, a scandalous rake; the third, a malicious intriguer; the fourth, and relatively most relishable of the company, Rabbi Markuse, is an amiable enough person and fairly well-conducted citizen, but childishly self-indulgent in little things and, although he poses as a modernized Nathan the Wise, a coward before public opinion. To show up by such farcical examples the wide discrepancy between profession and practice of the men of '48 is like waving the red flag in the faces of the survivors of the revolution. The other error, however, is of a still graver nature. In the fifth of the Fellow Stormers, Dentist Hartmeyer, who has the principal part, the old-time idealism burns on with undiminished fervor, and Sudermann, by making this one the most preposterous among the fantasts, with his objectless, querulous enthusiasm and quixotic lack of common sense, lays a hurtful finger on a very sensitive spot in the national consciousness of his countrymen. The German people are rightly

proud of their idealism. It is bad form and bitterly unjust for Sudermann to hold up the old
ideals of '48 to the scorn of the modern generation. It is difficult to see what good turn can be
served either the human or the national cause by
a political comedy which seems to point out the
harrowing lesson that democracy is half villainy,
half folly. And the representatives of the new
epoch, the sons of the Fellow Stormers, being with
one exception contemptible and vicious, are not
calculated to show that vigorous ideals of any sort,
old or new, serve as lodestars for the guidance
of the men who are young to-day in Imperial Germany. One might condone the pessimism shown
in the historical retrospect in spite of its indiscreet expression. *Der Katzensteg* contained the
proof that such dissent from the generally accepted
patriotic tradition may go hand in hand with a
confidence in the existence of a truly efficacious
national idealism. But to judge from *Der Sturmgeselle Sokrates* it almost looks as though, in a
fit of disgust, Sudermann had shifted his moral
perspective. To the defense raising its faint voice
here and there and offering the objection that
Der Sturmgeselle Sokrates must not be received
as an attack on cherished national ideals there

is but one answer. The ethics of every drama must stand trial on their plain appearances, nothing else.

After this outspoken condemnation of Sudermann's latest play a warning will be in place that we should not lend a serious ear to his obdurate detractors. It would simplify the study of a great writer if ethical and æsthetic development were necessarily following a straight line up or down. As a rule, however, great writers are so constituted or circumstanced that an occasional slipping back from their path of ascent or a not too frequent recrudescence into a past phase of endeavor need not be taken as a symptom of decay. We must let them take their own time and their own way to reach the summit of their art. Thus as in conclusion we sum up the results of Sudermann's work during this decade and a half of his rich literary activity, we may in good faith eliminate from the estimate the two or three books that are distinctly inferior in value to the rest of the imposing series.

The art of Hermann Sudermann, notwithstanding the range of its capabilities, is fundamentally simple in its character. Its purpose is direct, its form clearly defined, incisive, at times lapidary.

It is an art that reposes on a well-poised, full-orbed, full-veined personality. His failures refute the groundless charge that Sudermann truckles to the dominant literary taste of the hour. He fashions from a deep artist's conscience and out of the fullness of a strong outspoken temperament. Again and again he has been reviled as a mechanical imitator of the French *salon*-dramatists. It is perfectly certain and greatly to his credit that he has learned much from older and contemporary masters, both in respect to the general principles and the minor managements of dramatic art. Why should not an artist, in order to reach a higher position, mount on the shoulders of eminent predecessors? It is not true, however, that Sudermann has schooled his craftsmanship exclusively after the French pattern. The fact is, he studied in the same places as most of his competitors, but he has proved himself an apter pupil. To Ibsen and Björnson he owes probably more than to any other living writers for the technic, the subject-matter, and even the ethics of his works. Undoubtedly he has, besides, acquired constructive details from the older school of French dramatists, maybe he has also been influenced by them in giving room to some of those

things which for the lack of a better word we
must term with his detractors "theatricalities."
Spielhagen may be right in claiming for Count
Trast a lineal descent from the Count of Monte
Cristo. Yet with rare exceptions these "theatricalities" are not used as a claptrap for a gullible
public, for it should be remembered that Sudermann writes for a nation to whom the drama is
something far higher than a mere "show." They
are in all likelihood the spontaneous outflow of a
dramatic disposition. On the whole Sudermann
indulges with discretion his natural propensity for
the spectacular. As an instance, take the reception prepared for the prima donna Maddalena dall'
Orto (Magda) in a city which may constructively
be called Königsberg, the capital of East Prussia. The streets and houses are decked with gar-
lands, rugs, and flags; crowds surge in front of
her house, and so forth. These things do not
pass on the scene and therefore cannot enhance
the stage effect of the play, but they betray the
author's penchant for picturesque exaggeration to
which he yields now and then when he thinks
himself unobserved. Examples of the same kind
might easily be multiplied. Theatrical rather than
dramatic are likewise the ablegates, as we have

called them, or mouthpieces of the author's private opinion. In the novels as well as in the plays there is a superfluity of speech-making and other declamation. There is also in both kinds of works a regular return of the "grand scene." But these things which fly in the face of naturalism do not constitute, as the enemies would have it, a cardinal dramaturgic vice of Sudermann. They merely prove that he aspires to no high place among the naturalists.

A play or a novel may be lifelike without being true to life. Sudermann is less concerned with external accuracy than with internal truth. The things which he depicts on the stage and in the pages of his books are not soulless copies from life, nor yet are they, on the other hand, mere inventions of the imagination. They are fragments of his own inner experience, composed and interpreted for others. Herein consists the convincing power of his art. He has had the courage from the beginning to brave the naturalistic despotism, and to hold out for the conviction that, as Amiel has it in his *Journal intime*, "the ideal, after all, is truer than the real; for the ideal is the eternal element in perishable things: it is their type, their sum, their *raison d'être*, their formula in the book of

the Creator, and therefore at once the most exact
and the most condensed expression of them."
For this reason it is that such figures as the plod-
ding Paul Mayhöfer, the robust Leo von Sellenthin, the feline Adah Barczinowsky, the blond
serpent Felicitas von Kletzing, or the roughshod,
blustering, golden-hearted Squire Vogelreuter,
and many another figure of Sudermann's are
more than ephemeral creations. They are lasting contributions to the history of contemporary morals and manners, and therefore may be
fairly ranked with such imperishable products
of the writer's art as Captain Dobbin, Rawdon
Crawley, the Marquis of Steyne, or even the in-
comparable Becky Sharp herself. Though com-
parisons in the domain of literature are especially
odious, yet one feels strongly tempted to spin out
somewhat further the comparison between Sudermann and England's greatest novelist, Thackeray.
The stinging lash swung by both is in appointed
hands; it is wielded by righteous indignation in
the name of a higher morality. And that is good
additional reason why we pardon Sudermann's
occasional undramatic preachments. He is not
an artist for art's sake alone; he is also a vigorous
reformer. Yet again like Thackeray, he is not

perpetually plying the scourge of scathing sarcasm. He is also richly endowed with real benig-
nant humor, a gift of the gods which no great
writer can spare, and one which can make even
an out-and-out realist almost endurable.

The art of Sudermann is simple also in that it
applies itself almost invariably to a single group
of problems. The keynote to the great majority
of his works is the world-old conflict which is
daily bred anew in the life of a progressive people:
the tragic struggle between the old and the new;
between the pious clinging of the soul to long-
recognized creeds and the imperious claims of a
nascent era.

In his attitude towards these grave questions
Sudermann is consistently conservative so far as
the general status of society is concerned; he is
liberal, radical, nay anarchistic, in his pleas for
special cases. Yet he is not stubbornly marking
time on the standpoint of any one doctrine. We
find, on the contrary, in his dramatic career the
evidences of a growing, maturing, and refining
philosophy. Roughly speaking, three phases may
be distinguished. At first, the class conflict *per se*
is in the foreground, the fates of the individuals
are of secondary interest. The type of these

dramas is *Die Ehre*. In that play the final destinies of Robert and Lenore, Alma and Kurt, are disposed of with a nonchalant wave of the hand. The most interesting part of *Die Ehre* is the perambulating social commentary of the author, here represented by the Count von Trast-Saarberg.

It is not long, however, before the major sympathies of Sudermann are transferred from the sociologic class phenomena in the abstract to the concrete, living individual. The first play of this second phase is " Magda." The connection with the teachings of Friedrich Nietzsche is obvious. The highest duty of the exceptional type is to cultivate its true genius, regardless of the statutes and by-laws of society. The exceptional man or woman must therefore follow the pathfinding instinct. Such is the prime consideration. The most sacred bonds must be severed as soon as they become a hindrance to the free unfolding of individuality. At the same time, genius may not, after defying the conventions and thus securing its own higher form of happiness, expect to participate with equal shares in the happy lot of the throng. Thus every genius is placed in the ancient Sapphic dilemma.

There is a third class of plays by Sudermann
representing a yet higher stage of ethical conception. A person may be at the same time sovereignly independent and sovereignly unselfish.
Teja is an apotheosis of civic martyrdom, *Johannes*
a glorification of the gospel of love. Marikke, too,
and Beate in their way show their strength not so
much in self-assertion as in self-abnegation.

And it may be that Sudermann as an ethicist
has not yet spoken his final and decisive word.
At any rate, so far as his social plays are concerned, his work up to the present time shows
him only twice as the reckless satirist, in *Sodoms
Ende*, where he puts profligacy into the pillory,
and in *Der Sturmgeselle Sokrates*, meant as a
warning either against false idealism or against
want of idealism. At all other times Sudermann
maintains the helpful attitude of a sober, determined reformer. He handles his chosen problems
not, as so many modern writers do, for the sake
of pleasing the caprice of a frivolous public, nor
to gratify any morbid curiosity or idiosyncrasy of
his own, but because they have come to distinct
public consciousness, and because he personally
is deeply stirred by them. As a novelist he has
reached true greatness. In the drama he falls

short of it because his strong pedagogic bent warps his plots from their natural course, not letting fate arise wholly out of the characters, and because, moreover, in his plays the horizon of the "idea" and the circle of action are not always coextensive.

Nevertheless, if we have outgrown that pedantic narrowness which approves or disapproves of a writer in proportion as he happens to agree or disagree with our own views of things, and if in judging him we turn from the sundry crudities and blemishes of which hardly any work of art can be wholly free, and fix our attention on his honest aims and high merits, we shall gladly acknowledge Hermann Sudermann as one of the foremost exponents of the modern novel and drama.

MODERN
GERMAN LITERATURE

GERHART HAUPTMANN

GERHART HAUPTMANN

A census taken at any time during the past decade or so to determine whom the present generation regards as the greatest living dramatist of Germany would result beyond a peradventure in the overwhelming triumph of Gerhart Hauptmann.

How much this well-nigh unanimous judgment may portend for Hauptmann's ultimate position in German and European literature, how much or how little warrant there is for already assigning to him a well-defined historic personality, will be a matter for speculation until the literary or cultural movement to which his works and his fame owe their origin shall have receded from the field of blurred contemporaneous vision and appear to the eye in the distinctness of historic perspective.

On the other hand, there can be no doubt that the general appreciation of Hauptmann signifies for our own time the victorious penetration of certain æsthetic principles into the art conception

of a vast majority of the Germans. These principles, which may be summed up in the well-
known term " naturalism," came into vogue, so
far as Germany is concerned, about fifteen years
ago, at first among a small group of young writers.
Before they had spread so widely as finally to win
for the new art gospel wide circles of society high
and low, they had undergone a number of modifi-
cations, the leading writers of the school passing
through an almost radical change in their artistic
conviction.   It is evident to us at this distance
that the extreme naturalism of Hauptmann's first
play in 1889 represents merely a played-out episode in the consistent movement of the modern
drama towards greater truthfulness. The abiding
service of naturalism to the higher realism into
which it is now merged consists in the accomplished reunion of dramatic art with actual life
after a long and disastrous period of separation.
In its results this reunion means no less than
that the theater to-day occupies in the national
consciousness of the Germans a place such as
throughout the history of mankind it has been
known to command only once before, at the time
when Greek tragedy was in its flower. To convert a place for the entertainment of the well-to-do

lazy into a serious institution for the deepening of the public art intelligence it was needful to work a series of reforms. Already the method had been laid out by Emile Zola in his *Le Roman expérimental*, by which the epic form of letters was to be brought into an organic touch with life. By the same or a closely similar prescription the drama was now to be remade. The naturalists felt that the drama should be a reproduction of the actual, unaltered by any embellishment or idealistic additions of any kind. Hence it is necessary to learn to observe the actual in a scientific way; and as the phenomena under scrutiny are manifestations of organic life, the naturalistic dramatist should strive to fathom them by methods akin to those employed in the biologic pursuits. However, the most painstaking registration of data does not produce a drama, because the social processes are too composite and slow-working for the limited possibilities of the stage, and too subtle for the offhand comprehension of the public. So, by analogy of natural science, the dramatists segregate relatively small groups of factors and study experimentally their mutual reactions. This at least is their theory, and here is not the place to combat the fallacy which it harbors.

Two corollaries of this alleged scientific method have to be mentioned: The "passion of veracity" implies the preponderance of the commonplace in the looks and acts of the characters and notably in their speech, and thus makes among other things the use of dialect and jargon indispensable. The environment of each individual must be accurately rendered; hence a mass of epic detail is conveyed through the medium of stage directions, which thus become an intrinsic part of the play. It was on the perfection of these and other technical matters that naturalism at first took its stand; the higher object of the drama was wholly submerged under its minutiæ.

This higher object for the naturalist was to show through a multiplicity of examples that man's destiny is unalterably shaped by his inherited character in conjunction with his environment; human fate proceeds from a parallelogram of forces extrinsic rather than volitional. So much, in passing, for the naturalistic creed. However, even the author of *Le Roman expérimental,* the gospel of the naturalists, had declared that art is a segment of the world seen through a temperament. In truth, the temperamental or subjective coloring can never be absent from a work of art.

So far as it goes, it will set apart the work of one writer from the work of all others. For this reason we find that with his peculiarly lyric temperament it is no easy task for Hauptmann, even in the beginning of his career as a dramatist, to conform strictly to the tenets of the new art code, and that occasionally he breaks away altogether from allegiance to the school.

In the preceding chapter Sudermann was described as a writer of the masculine type. Hauptmann is the opposite. Sudermann's pen is guided by a theory of life. Hauptmann apparently has not yet evolved one for himself. Whenever he departs from the visible model and follows either an imaginative or a speculative bent, it at once becomes apparent that his poetry is not moored to a definite, consistent philosophy. Hauptmann as a thinker, say in *Einsame Menschen* or *Die versunkene Glocke*, is handicapped by the same intense impressibility that enables him in *Die Weber* or *Der Biberpelz* to show among all his contemporaries the greatest skill in the art of accurate and minute *milieu* painting. The specific nature of his prodigious lyric gifts, notably the lilting melody of his verse, which so often asserts itself triumphantly over the doctrinal veto, springs from a decadent predisposition. The much-abused word decadent is to be taken not at all in a sinister meaning, but to denote a state of overrefinement manifesting itself in a subtle yet sterile receptivity, brooding pensiveness, and — perhaps the chief criterion — in a certain debility of the volitional energy, which leaves this poet in a condition of tormenting doubt on major questions of life, and which even in his pursuit of an art ideal makes him seem vacillating and visionary. Hauptmann, too, is apparently as incapable of the higher self-discipline as are his heroes. With his peculiar mental and temperamental equipment he might well have become the foremost lyrist of his generation. When he leaves free rein to his poetic fancy (as here and there already in *Hannele* and throughout *Die versunkene Glocke*) he gives being to poems of exquisite beauty, veritable asphodel blossoms, fragrant with a delicate and melancholy sweetness.

More than that, there is a fine lyric quality in all of Hauptmann's plays, a *Stimmungszauber* unmatched by any other modern dramatist; even the most crassly naturalistic among them, *Vor Sonnenaufgang*, contains one such scene of great beauty. In this power of drawing the spectator

at will into the mood of the play lies Hauptmann's real strength. It is not, however, for his
lyric genius but as a dramatist pure and simple
that Hauptmann is worshiped by his contemporaries. And with the exception of an epic
(later withdrawn from the book market), a few
desultory novel fragments, a number of wholly
unknown poems, and a couple of short stories, his
published work consists of a long and altogether
remarkable series of plays. Like most continental
writers of to-day Hauptmann craves the quick
and tumultuous response of the living generation.
This may be secured only in the theater. So
Hauptmann writes plays, and through a natural
fallacy of public opinion he has been proclaimed
Germany's greatest living dramatist. Yet it may
be severely questioned whether he should be
considered for that place of honor. A dramatic
writer may be a great poetic genius and an indifferent maker of plays. Had Goethe given
us nothing else but *Faust* we should nevertheless accord him readily the first position among
modern poets; but should we in that case be
justified in calling Goethe the greatest modern
dramatist just because *Faust* is cast in the
dramatic form?

Judged by a just dramaturgic standard, Hauptmann is deficient in three essentials. In the first
place, he is weak as regards his dynamics. The
characters are stationary, incapable of any real
development. In a certain way they are very true
to life, thanks to their author's prodigious power of
observation and his absorbing attention to detail.
They are gotten up regardless of pains. Not the
wart on the nose, not the speck of dust on the
coat, is overlooked. Of the very definite impression their prototypes have made on his eye,
Hauptmann renders such accurate account that
when his men and women make their first appearance their verisimilitude elicits our highest admiration. After a while, however, the interest in
them flags, owing to their persevering sameness.
Neither literally nor figuratively do they ever
change their clothes. They evolve no new ideas
from within, they admit none from the outside,
and they never relent in their stubborn adherence
to what ideas they happen to possess. The original stock, moreover, with which the author has
set them up is so limited as to constitute another
weakness of Hauptmann's plays. For truth to tell,
the characters are wanting in ideas chiefly because
the author has not much of this commodity to

spare. Now fixed ideas are a dangerous equipment in proportion as they are few in number,
and one is tempted to think that the characters
in Hauptmann's plays meet their defeat through
their own unyielding devotion to the single fixed
idea that forms the dramatic viaticum of each.
To come to the third defect : Upon the glorious
authority of the ancients and of Shakespeare, we
feel justified in demanding of a dramatist that in
manipulàting a theme of his own deliberate choice
he shall turn his subject-matter to full account
and make the most of the dramatic data it presents. Of this reasonable demand Hauptmann
falls short. He does not convert all his metal into
coin. His art is imposing but fragmentary. His
pieces are counterfeits of life, but for the greater
part they are not dramas ; each constitutes a series
of living pictures succeeding each other without
an inevitable causal connection, coming somehow
to a stop but often lacking finality.

Naturalism is obviously self-contradictory in
that it prohibits poetic eclecticism in the presentment, and at the same time relies upon the selec-
tive power of the playwright to pick from a
human history a few brief scenes that shall of
themselves coalesce into a full drama.

As a matter of fact, the plots of Hauptmann are structurally weak and do not even present a firm and definite outline. This may be a virtue in the eyes of some naturalists, yet the suspicion is strong that it is a virtue made of necessity.

Hauptmann is not primarily cut out for a dramatist. But there is a species of drama which is not at all conterminous with life, and in which a first-rate poet may excel even without any superior dramatic power. Over the domain of the fairy-tale play Hauptmann might wield an absolute sovereignty, were it not for that deep-seated lack of a consistent theory of life which debars him from interpreting the nature and destiny of man through symbolism of the grander stamp.

Hauptmann has up to this time given us fifteen specimens of his dramatic art. Obviously they belong to two essentially different, nay contradictory and hostile, spheres. Between these, however, they are not cleanly divided; for in several of the plays the attempt is made at least to bridge the chasm that separates the worlds of fact and figment. The first six plays, closing with *Kollege Crampton*, are patterned throughout after the extreme naturalistic precept. In *Hannele* the poet swerves aside from this path of unalloyed

naturalism or " verism," to return to it again tran-
siently in *Der Biberpelz* (" The Beaver Coat "). In
Die versunkene Glocke (" The Sunken Bell ") he
once more turns into another road and finds the
way, so it would seem, to the true sanctum of his
genius. But the half dozen plays that have followed " The Sunken Bell " are so evenly divided
between the realistic and the idealistic spheres
that it would be obviously unfair to regard Hauptmann either any longer as an obdurate disciple of
naturalism or as an apostate from its principles.
As to the form to be taken by his future works
we are not in entire darkness. Yet it is not easy
to derive his developmental curve from the analysis of his works in their chronological order, for it
is Hauptmann's habit to carry on simultaneously
several dramatic works, and the technic of each
is to a great extent predetermined by the æsthetic
convictions that swayed the author during the
nascent stage of the composition, which may lie
farther back than the actual beginnings of works
published earlier. However, when all is said, an
important distinction will be drawn between the
naturalism of the earliest plays, which poses as
its own excuse, and that of *Fuhrmann Henschel*,
Michael Kramer, and *Rose Bernd*, which has

become subservient to an ulterior psychological theme supplying to the play its real content. It is wisest to abstain from prophecy. This much, however, it seems safe to predict: Hauptmann will continue to exercise his double talent. He will take his material, on the one hand, from his own experience and acquaintance. Here the dramatis personæ will be imitations of life, without the playwright's deeming it necessary to return to the sickening coarseness of his first effort. On the other hand, he will sojourn from time to time in his beloved fairyland where he feels so much at home. At any rate, it is certain that he will continue to grow in independence and be bound down less and less by the narrow æsthetic code of " Youngest Germany."

Before passing under review the plays of Gerhart Hauptmann in the order of their publication, it seems appropriate to sketch briefly his early personal history previous to his recognition as the leading exponent of realistic drama in Germany. Gerhart Hauptmann was born in 1862 in Obersalzbrunn, a small Silesian watering place, where his father kept at one time the three principal hotels. The hotel keeper Siebenhaar in *Fuhrmann Henschel* is said to be modeled after

Hauptmann's father. The poet's grandfather on the paternal side, who was in his early years a poor linen weaver, also became a well-to-do innkeeper.[1] On the maternal side as well Hauptmann is a son of the people. In 1874 he was sent to the capital city of Breslau, where he attended the Realschule. To the disappointment of his father, whose business had taken an unprosperous turn, he proved an unsatisfactory student, so that three years later it seemed wise to take him from school and try to make him turn his attention to agriculture. Soon he returned to Breslau, this time to study art, for which he had displayed a promising talent. His chronic rebellion against the discipline of the Royal Art School brought his connection with that institution to an early close. Although not qualified, technically, to enter a university, he was by special act admitted as a student of history at Jena. He was then, at twenty years of age, undecided between following the fine arts or literature as his vocation, and remained in this state of indecision for a number of years. After a few semesters at the university we find him at work, now in his sculptor's studio at Rome,

[1] In this connection it deserves to be noticed, perhaps, that the poet is a "total abstainer" and a professed enemy of strong drink.

now in Germany, drawing and modeling from life. Then again he discovered a still more congenial calling and entered upon a course of conscientious preparation to become an actor. This purpose he had to give up, partly because of an inability to overcome the lisp in his speech. In the meantime he had married, and by his wife's considerable fortune was freed from the anxieties of breadwinning and the necessity for compromise which poverty is so apt to impose on the artist. From 1885 began his relations with the rising literary generation, — he had removed to a place in the vicinity of Berlin, — and about that time also began his career as a writer. Of his first efforts but little has been preserved. As far as can be judged from fragments and snatches, they were not fundamentally at variance with the established literary routine against which his later works were to furnish such a vigorous protest. Therein lies probably one reason why Hauptmann has repudiated these utterances of his early apprenticeship. But most likely the principal reason is the low opinion the author now holds of the artistic worth of those firstlings of his genius. In a lengthy epic poem entitled *Promethidenlos* (" The Fate of the Children of Prometheus ") he recorded the variegated impressions and experiences of a voyage from Hamburg along the western coast of Europe and through the Mediterranean. He had journeyed in the tracks of "Childe Harold," and beyond a doubt his own poem is strongly colored by Byron. The epic, published in 1885, was soon withdrawn from circulation. The few copies that have not been remade into pulp are now high-priced curios of the book world. A collection of lyrics, *Das bunte Buch* ("The Motley Book"), had got as far as the page proof when the obscure publisher went into bankruptcy. The few samples cited by Hauptmann's biographer, Paul Schlenther, are not especially calculated to deepen our regret at the suppression of these verses. Not all, however, are as hopelessly commonplace as the one which commences with the best-known line of Heinrich Heine:

> Ich weiß nicht, was soll es bedeuten,
> Daß meine Träne rinnt
> Zuweilen, wenn ferne das Läuten
> Der Glocke, der Glocke beginnt.

In 1889 Hauptmann formed the acquaintance of Arno Holz. Holz impressed him very much with his clear, incisive analysis of the literary conditions, and gave him the final impetus towards "realism," Hauptmann for some time having strongly tended in that direction. Holz and his equally talented friend, Johannes Schlaf, were the joint authors of a number of photographically lifelike sketches named *Papa Hamlet*, after an old play actor who is the subject of the leading story in the collection. This book seemed then to Hauptmann the very acme of consistent naturalism. The lesson it taught him he valued so highly that he dedicated his own first realistic play, which appeared soon after, to " Bjarne P. Holmsen," which was the partnership pen name of Holz and Schlaf. This play of Hauptmann's is called *Vor Sonnenaufgang* (" Before Sunrise "). It appeared in book form in the summer of 1889 and was first performed under the auspices of the *Freie Bühne* (" The Free Theater," a private organization not harassed by censorship) on October 20 of the same year. From this play, which at once divided the play-going public into two camps, dates Hauptmann's fame. Its plot and manner of presentation struck the audience dumb with admiration or aroused it to an indignant protest, according to the literary party allegiance confessed by each person present at the performance. Fifteen years have passed since that time;

in Germany the extreme naturalism for which *Vor Sonnenaufgang* supplied the paradigm has run its course, but as the United States participates so little in the literary movements that sway the European intellect, the contents of *Vor Sonnenaufgang* may still be a novelty to most American readers. I must state at the outset that in sketching out the contents of Hauptmann's first play I shall be obliged to pass over more than one important detail out of deference to the conventional laws of decorum.

Through the discovery of a rich coal seam in his land Farmer Krause becomes unexpectedly a very rich man. He forthwith conceives some mild social ambitions for his family, to gratify which he marries his elder daughter to a civil engineer and sends the younger to a Moravian boarding school. Not being ambitious on his own account, he proceeds to indulge his one congenital passion,—a ceaseless craving for alcohol. His normal condition is that which with characteristic injustice toward the dumb animals we call a state of beastly drunkenness. Let the quotation-worn slander for once be repudiated. Even Mr. Thompson-Seton, who surely knows stranger things about the wild animals than

philosophy and natural history e'er dreamt of,
would agree that no animal lower than man
revels in such degradation as Farmer Krause.
The precious home circle over which this hopeless sot presides includes his infamous rake of
a son-in-law, Hofmann. A choice quartet is completed by Krause's hopelessly depraved wife and
her cicisbeo, a lecherous hostler. Into this delightful company the younger daughter, Helene,
a girl of education and fine feelings, is thrown
on her return from school. She could hardly be
expected to feel at home in it. The clammy,
reeking filth of her surroundings, pressing forward and onward round her, must needs darken
her pure girlhood. Her heart loudly counsels
her to fly from the importunities of her amorous
brother-in-law as well as from other evils — but
whither? She loves Alfred Loth, a socialist so
stanch that he has spent two years in jail for
the sake of his convictions. Is this for Helene
the call of fate? Almost it would seem so, as
Loth returns her love. But it avails naught,
for Loth under his hygienic flannel shirt is the
possessor of a coarse-grained socialist conscience
and peremptory principles. Like most men of
his political faith, he has read an alarming deal.

Accordingly he has, among other things, very
decided views on marriage; to put it shortly, to
him no daughters of tainted parents need apply.
Without losing much time over the customary
conflict bred of such a predicament, Loth gives
up Helene. The socialist dogma is safe! And in
order, probably, to save herself from an unspeakable assault by her own ribald father, Helene stabs
herself to death — Before Sunrise.

There are not many books in the literature of
the world which spread about them an atmosphere so reeking with vice and horror as this
socialistic drama. Tolstoi's *The Power of Darkness* and Zola's *L'Assommoir* and *La Terre* are
its nearest of kin. But even these, in spite of
their dread aspect, do not present such a spectacle of condensed hideousness. A confirmed
drunkard committing suicide — at the age of
three! a father who lusts after his own daughter!
(When we encounter such things, do we not feel
like apologizing to Dr. Alfred Loth for our
sentimental disapproval of his course towards
Helene?) the distressing cries of a woman in
labor issuing from an adjacent room! — for the
full-fledged "naturalist" physiological details like
these have no horrors: it is otherwise with the

spectator. When after coming home from the
revolting entertainment he has thoroughly dis-
infected himself by a hot tubbing, a man will
naturally ask, Does such a degenerate assortment of the species man have any place on
the foreground of the stage? Granted that the
play is " true "; for it will not do to affirm, as has
been done by the unsophisticated, that such
scum of society does not really exist, because
forsooth Rosegger and Anzengruber, Auerbach
and Fritz Reuter have portrayed peasant life in
such different colors; or that such pest-holes as
Farmer Krause's home are never found in rural
parts, and that *Vor Sonnenaufgang* is the product of a pure culture of rustic vice raised by
Hauptmann in the coziness of his Berlin work-
room. Still we may in fairness inquire of the
naturalist, Why this surfeit of ugliness when life
is not ugly *a potiori?* Or are we to believe that
the Krauses and their tribe form not an exception but the rule? In such a case what were
there left for us city dwellers to do but wage
a holy war against all country folk? The language of the drama is as disgusting as the incidents; in no other play has Hauptmann sinned
so unpardonably against common decorum, for

he soon realized that the naturalistic method can be applied to a higher order of social processes.

The foregoing must not for a moment be taken as an unduly biased judgment. Nothing could be more alien to the spirit of this book than factious or dogmatic opposition to "modernism." Hauptmann's *Vor Sonnenaufgang*, however, was felt to be an overdose which the moderns themselves could not altogether stomach. One of their chieftains, Conrad Alberti, burlesqued this sordid tragedy of gin and lust. His skit bears the alluring title *Im Suff* ("In Booze"), and the charming motto *Die Liebe und der Suff, das reibt den Menschen uff* (" Twixt love and booze, one goes to the deuce "). Hauptmann's pedantically circumstantial stage directions are capitally taken off. "Dr. Krawutschke" is thus presented to the reader: "He wears striped trousers, a checked jacket, and soiled linen. The left shoe is down at the heel, but not noticeably so. He speaks very rapidly in abrupt sentences, with a decided touch of the Saxon dialect (he was born in Scheffel Street, Dresden)." At the close Alberti makes the ghost of Lessing appear and say, " Is this a theater or a pigsty?" This product, coming from one of the apostles of the new art-creed, deserves attention if only for the sake of the epigram with which it dismisses the reader: "To befoul Art is not to free it" (*Die Kunst beschmutzen heißt nicht sie befrei'n*).

Such, then, was Hauptmann's first play. His next, *Das Friedensfest* ("The Feast of Peace") (1890) — the title is an abortive attempt at grim irony — deals not with the degeneration of a whole family, as *Vor Sonnenaufgang*, nor with any deep-reaching human depravity, but with the supposedly inevitable fate of a certain group of pathologically predisposed individuals who are thrown together as a family. Held against its predecessor, this play does not present any essentially new features. Again it has to do with a segment from a family history which, so far as it goes, unrolls itself in a series of imperfectly dovetailed scenes, although there is, all doctrinaire assertions to the contrary notwithstanding, not absent a constructive groundwork. Once more the havoc wrought by alcohol forms the foregone refrain of the sad old story. Once more we learn with dismay how loosely, according to a modern view, the bonds of family life

are tied, and how wantonly they are ruptured
by straining egoism. Fritz Scholz, M.D., and
Minna, by twenty-two years his junior, are part-
ners in an uncongenial marriage. The doctor, a
hypochondriac by constitution, takes it much to
heart that his wife fails to understand him. We
shall have occasion to observe that many of
Hauptmann's heroes keep him company in this
form of misery. Indeed, this failure to be understood, like the curse of alcohol, is one of the
fixed motives in his dramaturgy. In the present
instance the two are connected as cause and
effect in that Dr. Scholz seeks consolation in
winebibbing. Already we are sufficiently con-
versant with a third leitmotif, that of heredity,
to foresee that at least one of the children must
have a fondness for liquor. There are three of
them: a pinched old maid of a daughter and two
sons. Robert, aged twenty-eight, has the physical and moral earmarks of a degenerate; along
with a predilection for strong drink he owes to
his progenitor a morbid excitability; of his bodily
infirmities youthful dissipations are the direct
cause, but, naturally, the real blame for these
falls also on his ancestry. (At Jena Hauptmann
had become deeply interested in Darwinism, and

in his plays he frequently draws the bold infer-
ences characteristic of the layman.) The second
son, Wilhelm, aged twenty-six, has by virtue of
a powerful constitution escaped the consequences
of youthful excesses; but to prove that he also
has come in for his share in the patrimony, he
shows, besides a vehement temper, promising
symptoms of persecution-mania. While still very
young both boys had run away from the unbear-
able tyranny of the father and learned to shift for
themselves. Later the family was reunited, when
a terrible catastrophe again drove them apart.
In his unjustifiable jealousy of a visiting musician
old Dr. Scholz wrongfully accused his wife of
infidelity; for this he was punished by the hands
of his own younger son. He then left his home,
the sons following his example separately. This
chapter of history now six years old is unrolled
with great skill after the Ibsen fashion in the
course of the first act. The curtain rises on the
Christmas preparations of the Scholz household.
The festival of " Peace on Earth " brings a general family reconciliation. The father, who in the
meantime has undergone a severe nervous crisis,
returns unexpectedly and joins the reunited circle.
Wilhelm, in a scene of frightful pathos, receives

his father's forgiveness. His promised wife, Ida
Buchner, dispels by her firm love and confidence
his intermittent scruples about drawing her into
his sullied existence. So things look wholly aus-
picious to the unscientific observer. Suddenly,
and for no visible cause, jarring discords destroy
the precarious harmony and the family feud
breaks out afresh. The barely reconciled brothers
clash again; the father banishes the diabolic
Robert from his house, then relapses into his
mania and disappears (end of act ii) from the
scene. At the conclusion of the third act he dies.
The kindly, resolute Frau Buchner has had ample opportunity during her brief visit to repent
of her purpose to bring peace into the family so
haplessly torn by incessant strife; and we wonder greatly at her consent to the marriage between Wilhelm and Ida. The author apparently
feels obliged to account for her readiness, and he
does it strangely enough by showing that Frau
Buchner is, in the depths of her resigned heart,
herself in love with her daughter's betrothed
and more solicitous about his future happiness
than about her own daughter's. This fruitful
motive is not further exploited, nor is that other
world-old one of the rival brothers more than

suggested in the evident infatuation of Robert for his brother's fiancée. Towards the end Wilhelm suffers a rather telling attack of persecution-mania, which sets him thinking and again makes him waver in his resolution to marry Ida; but being without Alfred Loth's oversensitive conscience, he will marry all the same and take his chances on Ida's future happiness.

The play thus terminates in one of those large question marks with which the works and the heads of the modern school are so abundantly equipped.

The next play, *Einsame Menschen* (" Lonely Souls ") (1891), is better rounded out. Things are this time carried to a final issue in that the hero, Hans Vockerat, perishes after Hauptmann's favorite method — by suicide. Nevertheless, it is a question whether the definite problem of modern life which is here tackled in good earnest is fairly worked out. How, indeed, is such a thing possible without the use of psychologic resources? And we know that these are eschewed by the rigid naturalist!

What, then, is the theme of *Einsame Menschen?* The inner dissonance of a man torn betwixt religion and science, between the duties of son

and husband and the calling of the inner voice,
a struggle forsooth from which an unstable nature
like that of Johannes Vockerat may well seek
escape in death. Yet Hauptmann, by adding still
another pang to his hero's sufferings, has weak-
ened the probability of the tragic end. For be it
remembered that, dramatically speaking, only that
ending seems probable which we accept as necessary. And there is no compelling reason for
Johannes' drowning himself because the Russian
student Anna Mahr, for whom he has conceived a
crotchety sort of love, prepares to go out of his
life. The fact is, Johannes dies because from the
very beginning he is under irrevocable sentence of
death pronounced by the author, a decree which
furnishes the greatest weakness in *Einsame Menschen*. In all other technical respects the play
marks a considerable progress. In the first place,
the details of the new technic are now handled
with much greater freedom; consequently they
do not have to monopolize the author's attention.
He is at liberty to bestow greater care on the
larger features; and it must be said that *Einsame
Menschen* is one of the best-composed plays of the
modern stage. The events shape themselves with
a very fair show of natural, intelligent sequence.

Much critical capital has been made out of the resemblance of Hauptmann's piece to Ibsen's *Rosmersholm*. Undeniably Hauptmann has studied to good effect the style and method of the great Norwegian, and there is analogy in the situations too. To me the German play appeals as the truer of the two so far as the humanity of the characters goes. Psychologically these characters are certainly better founded than those in Hauptmann's own earlier plays, a circumstance which may safely be attributed to the author's better acquaintance with the social class to which they belong. When dealing with such people he descends, almost unintentionally, below the crust of appearances to the springs of action. Unfortunately the central situation is, as has been hinted, too calculated, too preëstablished, to be much affected by the better mind-reading powers of the author.

The simple action of *Einsame Menschen* revolves round one of those persons for whom Goethe discovered the appellation *Problematische Naturen* (problematic characters). Johannes Vockerat is studying to be a theologian, when through Darwin and Haeckel the drift of the modern scientific era is forcibly borne upon him. He forsakes theology and becomes a philosopher of the psycho-physiological school, though the old orthodox Adam is not quite dead within him. For years he has now been fretting over his prospective *magnum opus*. But it is safe to say he would never have achieved the work, even if Hauptmann's five-act tragedy had not effectually cut him off from the possibility, for he is a man with a broken will. We meet his brothers and cousins everywhere in Hauptmann's dramatic world. The family type is classically expressed in Master Heinrich of "The Sunken Bell" celebrity. Johannes loves his wife for a while and after a fashion; but when by chance he meets Anna Mahr he finds that she is more congenial to him. She understands him, and, mark well, he has never been understood before. So he falls in love with her, after a fashion, and now we behold him swinging to and fro between two poles of amatory attraction, just as he has all the time been the shuttlecock between the battledores of two opposite philosophies. His curse is indecision; his only stability is in his self-love, for Johannes Vockerat loves himself at all times and after every fashion. He talks a great deal about himself, a great deal about his work. Somehow he expects all the world to pave and smooth the way for it, and as its prospective author deems himself excused from all the practical obligations that fall to the head of a well-ordered family. When his poor, loving Käte meekly questions him regarding a vital business matter, he coarsely insults her for breaking in upon his valuable trend of thought. Explicitly he declares that he will regulate his conduct according to this formula: " My work comes first. That comes first and second and third; the 'practical' does not come until after that, if you please." A man with such a disposition is foredoomed either to a life of solitude or to a life of failure. There is enough misfortune in Johannes Vockerat's temperament without the supervention of a forbidden love. The troublous aspect of such Wertherian characters as Johannes was for a long time of absorbing interest to Hauptmann. He dedicated *Einsame Menschen* to those who " had lived through " the tragedy. And yet such conflicts as are here portrayed were then (1891) seemingly foreign to his personal experience. But this need not matter, perhaps, in any literary form save the lyric. *Einsame Menschen* bodies forth the experiences of another man, " observed," it is true, with a wonderful keenness, yet unfortunately not — in true poet fashion — relived by the dramatist. And so one could not help wishing that this highly gifted man might for once undertake a task the execution of which would vitally involve the coöperation of his own acquired experiences, or at least of deep-rooted, settled sympathies.

This opportunity offered itself in the naturalistic tragedy *Die Weber* (" The Weavers"), published in 1892, first performed in 1893, originally composed in dialect (*De Waber*), afterwards translated by the author into " literary " German with a still more than sufficient Silesian flavoring. This performance of Hauptmann's is replete with warmest personal feeling and wholly free from mere sentimental zeal, for he himself as the descendant of poor labor-driven linen weavers holds their grievance that cries to heaven as part and parcel of his heritage. From this personal participation in the wrongs perpetrated against the weavers the play derives a strong emotional swing, rising at times to the full height of rhetorical pathos, as in the impassioned tirade of Luise Hilse against the manufacturers. It was simply impossible for a subject that yielded so wide a space for personal feeling to be treated without a betrayal of the author's social creed. "The Weavers" is the tragedy of hunger driven at last to desperation. In Hauptmann's view the responsibility for the wretchedness of his proletarians rests evenly with the manufacturers because they carry on a ruthless scheme of spoliation, and with the state because it stands by and allows the merciless exploitation of the laborer. The workmen who now flock to the performances of *Die Weber* and wildly applaud its sentiment are very apt to forget that such a simple socialistic analysis of the case will hardly apply to conditions of to-day. That in some parts of the world there still exist such slave drivers as Herr Dreissiger (at first, after the original, he was called Zwanziger) is unfortunately not to be denied; but to regard such a man as the pattern of the propertied class would betray a perilous hastiness of judgment. At any rate, it is certainly unfortunate for the play that it owes its actual interest so largely to the fact that in it the antagonism which in a sufficiently acute form exists at all times between labor and capital here usurps the place of a concrete dramatic hero. In respect to dramatic movement this play is inferior to its predecessors. Each act brings a startlingly vivid scene of life, and yet the whole is unsatisfying to the dramatic sense. In the first act we are shown the cruelly realistic picture of an industrious, good-natured, withal stolidly patient people, brought low by grinding toil, and unable to live on its pitiful wage. Unfortunately Hauptmann has not exaggerated. The history of the "famine districts" of Silesia is even more grewsome than his dramatic tale. For nearly three centuries the weavers were fighting against starvation, and only once, in the summer of 1844,[1] they rose in frenzy against their masters. The rebellion was promptly suppressed before much damage had been done to anybody except the weavers.

About the middle of the past century the life that these poor folk of the Silesian "Eulengebirge" region led in fairly good times was unworthy of human beings. Their situation in hard times beggars description. Mother Baumert, whom a longish stage direction describes as accurately

[1] Gerhart Hauptmann became familiar with the details of that uprising through a special history written by Alfred Zimmermann, a political economist, who published in 1885 an exhaustive study of the conditions of the Silesian linen industry. But he had been touched much earlier by the sadness of their lot through stories current in his immediate family, and he declares in dedicating *Die Weber* to his father that the latter's story of his own father, who had passed his earlier life at the loom, was the real germ of his tragedy.

as though a warrant were out for her apprehension, gives a fair idea of their physical condition: " A face wasted to the bone, with folds and wrinkles in the bloodless skin; sunken eyes, watery and inflamed from the dust of the wool, smoke, and overwork by candlelight; a long, scrawny neck with a goiter; a hollow chest swathed in rags and tatters." In the second and third acts the spark of rebellion is carried among the down-trodden weavers from without. A son of the village, having served his military term in the city, returns, bringing with him the spirit of vengeance, and fires the weavers with enthusiasm for the " propaganda of action"; the bad gin from the tavern infuses additional courage, and they determine to settle accounts with their oppressors. In the fourth act the agitator is arrested and shackled, but on his way to prison he is rescued by the rioters from the grasp of the law, and the revolt breaks out in full force. Dreissiger's house is attacked and ravaged. The life of the usually so peaceful district is thrown into the wildest disorder. And so, at the end of the fourth act, the patent purpose of the tragedy is accomplished. There is no good reason why the author should not give the word right here for the royal musketry to rattle the death tattoo for the poor insurgents, since dramaturgically considered there can be no other way out of the chaos. There is, however, yet a fifth act, which practically constitutes a separate play; for the affecting death of God-fearing old Hilse, who to the end refuses to take part in the riot, is not tragic in the sense of dramatic art, rather it seems a satire on the injustice of fate that the poor fellow is killed by a stray bullet at his loom just when he has so stoutly declared: " Here my heavenly Father has placed me. . . . Here we are going to sit and do what's our duty," etc. Any one whose critical sense is not entirely blunted by the woeful distress which, as a unique motive with variations, dominates the action from beginning to end, feels, as the curtain finally hides the undying misery from his view, that this play more than any other work of Hauptmann's pen shows that its author follows the drama without a genuine dramatic vocation. Such as it is, without a hero to whom as to the natural center the interest might chiefly gravi-tate, without a more than inferential solidarity of its parts, with its final violent severance of the threads and filaments of the plot, " The Weavers" has aside from its vivacious realism chiefly a humanitarian value; it is, drawn out into five long acts, the blood-curdling outcry of an outraged class of society, who, lacking the leadership of a superior intelligence which might help them to strike off their shackles for good, allow themselves to follow shortsighted ringleaders and to vent their just anger in acts of wanton, insensate destruction, forthwith to acknowledge with thanks the drastic lesson given them by the ruling powers, and under the accustomed yoke to drag on the old calamitous existence.

Its power to draw forth deep human sympathy is the prime reason why this tragedy, despite its slenderness of incident and its technical shortcomings, has established Hauptmann in public opinion as the foremost tragic writer of Germany. And to be sure, for those who have to resort to the theater for instruction regarding the naked facts of common life, or for those who need to be dosed with a literary quintuple extract of human misery because their dyspeptic consciences fail to react under the stimulus of natural aliment, — for such " The Weavers" might pass for the very acme of creative power. And as for those who in their own lives have gone through the misery which " The Weavers" demonstrates *ad oculos*,

the impression made by the tragedy upon them
is so self-explanatory that we need not find fault
with the censor because, paternally solicitous for
the common weal, he failed to fling wide the
gates of the playhouses for "The Weavers."[1]   He
may have remembered, in these days of labor
troubles, that in the good old time the estimable
and worshipful aldermen of Leipzig canceled the
permit for the presentation of Schiller's "The
Robbers" during the annual Fair held in that
ancient and honorable town on the ground that
there would be enough stealing done at this time
anyway.   In forming an unbiased estimate of
Hauptmann's play, we should not be deceived
by its eloquent plea for the submerged portion
of humanity into ascribing the deep impression
infallibly produced by "The Weavers" to any
artistic superexcellence.   Hauptmann, to modify a
charge once made by Nietzsche against Richard
Wagner, entices us into the theater with the
promise of a dramatic entertainment, and once
he has us securely pinned down into our seats,
proceeds so to crush us with the force of a severe

---

[1] The performance is now licensed in Germany. (See p. 150.) Yet in
this country, if I mistake not, the anarchist John Most was enjoined
from playing the piece.

lecture that we forget everything except the elo-
quently presented rights and wrongs of the case.

Structurally "The Weavers" is below the standard of the earlier dramas. As for the diction,
Hauptmann still keeps under strict restraint that
glorious power of expression by which in his
later works he won universal admiration. In his
endeavor to make the people talk just as they
would in real life, he resists unyieldingly each and
every suggestion of stylistic improvement offered
by his better artistic sense. Undeniably he is a
master of the mean language of the people. Yet
the confusing jargon and the copious billingsgate
fall strangely from such refined lips. Even now
occasionally, in minor ways, we see the irrepress-
ible lyrist gain the upper hand, so that we are
not wholly unprepared to find the poet giving
full rein to his lyric genius in later works.

The play, even in its "German" translation,
loses much through the broad Silesian twang;
the relentless accuracy of the naturalist partially
defeats its own end when we can only with difficulty make out the speeches of his characters.
Die Weber has to do with a very much lower
stratum of society than either *Das Friedensfest* or
Einsame Menschen, both of which plays were

wholly free from grossness and smut. We are therefore prepared for rather strong things to happen in the speech and doings of these Pariahs of German society; and the author does not disappoint the expectation. To his honor be it said that Hauptmann is one of the most clean minded of men, and that he has never, not even in " Before Sunrise," been a cultivator of the revolting and obscene from sinister motives. While he is undoubtedly very open to the prepotent currents in the literary taste of his countrymen, owing to his exquisitely susceptive nature, he is, so far as his intentions go, swayed by no mercenary design upon the flippancy and sensational proclivities of the theater-goers. On the other hand, he does not recoil before any ugliness so long as he believes it to be helpful in the dramatic revelation of truth. It seems to me, however, that in " The Weavers," as in " Before Sunrise," he oversteps the limits of the permissible. In the second act we are forced to witness the preparations for the Baumert family's festive dinner. For two years these poor people have had no taste of meat. The roast that is now sizzling on their pan represents the mortal remains of the pet dog. Of this we are informed through our eyes, ears,

and noses, nay we are not even spared full knowledge of the disgusting consequences which the
unwonted reception of animal diet has for Father
Baumert's enfeebled stomach. I do not think
that reportorial conscientiousness need go to such
length. Reportorial conscientiousness is said advisedly, for unfortunately Hauptmann cannot be
accused of exaggeration.[1]

The two short stories, or "novelistic studies,"
as they are called by the author, *Bahnwärter
Thiel* ("Flagman Thiel"), written in 1887, and
Der Apostel ("The Apostle"), written in 1890,
may be conveniently mentioned in this place, as
they were published together in book form very
shortly after "The Weavers" (1892).

"Flagman Thiel" is unquestionably influenced
by Zola, and inspired by Hauptmann's sympathy
for the spiritual life of the lowly, which is so
pronounced in the dramas from "The Weavers"
on to his last production, the infanticide tragedy
Rose Bernd. It is the tragic story of a poor
railroad hand who marries a second time for the
sake of his idolized boy. The stepmother, a
coarse, violent, brutal wench, maltreats the little
fellow atrociously. Thiel, who returns only at

[1] See pp. 151 f.

fixed times from his post in the woods, and who, besides, is under the power of his new wife, is long ignorant of the true state of things. When he discovers it he loses all balance. His spiritual disintegration from that moment on to his total collapse over the accidental death of little Tobias and the maniacal killing of the wife and baby is the chief object of the "study." Not only is this object so well attained as by itself to cause a lively regret that the author has not essayed the epic form more frequently; Hauptmann also reveals, as indeed was to be confidently expected in view of his plays, a rare descriptive gift. The wonderful description of the nocturnal loneliness of a landscape gradually set aquiver and afire by the approach of the train is a marvel of loving observation. It is not the conventional onomatopœic rhapsody of the puffing and panting engine, the clash and clatter of the wheels and rails; nor the picture of the soulless monster painted so often, perhaps best by Emile Zola in *Bête humaine,*— or of the vitalized machine which from literary over-use has a touch of the stereotypic, even in Kipling's capital ".007." Hauptmann's nature-sense seizes upon the finest nuances of light and sound. The music of the whirring telegraph wires, the rhythmic welcome sung by the steel tracks and gradually changing into deafening turmoil is caught to perfection. Still more entrancing is the truly realistic and none the less highly poetic depiction of the light-effects. It is a pity that so drastic a power of description must seek its usual outlet in the minion and nonpareil of stage directions.

Der Apostel gives still wider space to the genius of Hauptmann. Written about the time when the first three plays were completed, it sounds almost like the signal of deliverance from naturalism. Hauptmann tries in this study to fathom a finely susceptible but mystically attuned soul gliding by degrees from an exalted religious mood into religious paranoia. Here again he is not without a literary model. The sketch of the poet Lenz by George Büchner serves him as such. And a living model, too, was in his mind : the religious eccentric, Johannes Gutzeit. The fragment shows the "Apostle," who was formerly an army officer, in the early morning hour, passing white robed through the streets of Zürich out into the country. In the presence of nature he experiences strange hallucinations and mysterious raptures. The fragment breaking off rather abruptly leaves the Apostle in the ecstatic belief that he is the Christ. This transition from a mere overwrought mental state to one of pronounced monomania is developed with consummate skill. Yet on the whole *Bahnwärter Thiel* deserves the prize over *Der Apostel*, since the latter is in fact only a "study," while the former presents itself as a finished "short story."

The next drama shows Hauptmann still firmly clinging to naturalism and striking up again his favorite tune, the old yet ever new song of King Alcohol. The central figure in *Kollege Crampton* ("Colleague Crampton") (1892) is a talented painter, who has fallen into evil and idle ways, and to whom the whisky bottle has to make amends for all blighted hopes and stunted or shattered ideals. In briefest terms his misfortunes may be diagnosed as congenital instability aggravated by domestic woes. At any rate, from the beginning to the end of the play he is a tipsy buffoon and a bankrupt financially, morally, and artistically. The action of the comedy begins on the morning when the reigning duke inspects the art academy where Colleague Crampton (one cannot help wondering why) is still tolerated as a teacher. Crampton, to whom the duke has formerly been very kind, sets extravagant hopes on this visit. The news that His Highness has left the school without so much as inquiring for him puts the good-natured idler utterly beside himself. Now blow upon blow follows in rapid succession. His wealthy wife leaves him, his goods are attached, he is asked to resign his professorship. He must leave his snug studio, the scene of his protracted inactivity; with full sail he sets his course towards his inevitable destination — the gutter. It must be added that Crampton divides his valuable affections between the aforementioned whisky bottle and his own lovely daughter, Gertrude. At the present juncture the whisky bottle accompanies him to cheer his exile, whereas the lovely daughter, who loyally sides with him against her mother, remains behind. She is befriended by Max Strähler (Strähler was the maiden name of Hauptmann's mother), a favorite pupil of Professor Crampton, who has been expelled from the academy because of foolish pranks (an experience which befell young Gerhart Hauptmann himself while an art student at Breslau), but who, out of gratitude to his former teacher, finds for the daughter a home among his relatives.

Up to this point we have before us the not
unskillful exposition of a piece which so far
secedes from the accepted code of dramaturgy
as to resist classification; judging by this part
of the play (acts i and ii) alone, one cannot say
for the life of him whether the plot makes for a
comedy or a tragedy. From here on things jog
along helter-skelter in the naturalistic groove, a
course of affairs which does not prevent the
remaining acts from bristling with improbabili-
ties. For instance, one whole act is taken up
with Max's fruitless search for the whereabouts
of the jolly old reprobate. We are expected to
believe that in a German town of medium size
a well-known inhabitant can disappear as quickly
and effectually as the proverbial needle in the
haystack. Adolf Strähler, Max's older brother, is
too sensible to believe as the audience must, and
discovers the hiding place of the missing artist
without any trouble. In the third act Crampton pops up in a wretched pothouse, hopelessly
befuddled, having during all that time assiduously soaked his ever thirsty soul. Here at the
head of a delegation of merry-making philistines
a master house painter makes Crampton, in good
faith and with due modesty, the generous offer

of permanent and fairly well paying work. Well,
why not? Many a better man in Crampton's
situation has found himself face to face with a
similar proposition, and ofttimes the offer has not
been scorned. Yet the author of " Colleague
Crampton" would have us believe that the
painter's harmless though clumsy suggestion is
rank arrogance and hollow mockery, and that it
conveys an insult so awful that even a Crampton is almost sobered by it. In what — we might
then appeal from Crampton drunk to Crampton
sober — does the honest fellow's crime consist?
Is his trade in itself dishonoring? Or does he
intend through this offer to lower Crampton's
genius in the eyes of the world? Or are we to
regard the scene as symbolic of the sad yoking
of the artist's genius by an unfeeling, commer-
cialized age? Certainly this would be reading
into the play more of tendency than were good
for its realism! And, by the way, how do we
know that Crampton is a real genius? Must we
appraise him at his own estimate?

The above incident marks the tip of the ascend-
ing action. Immediately afterward Max appears,
pays the debts of his future father-in-law, — for
this relationship he has diligently prepared the

way, — and, having secretly bought up the auc-
tioned possessions of the professor, piece by
piece, leads him in the last act back to the new
studio, furnished precisely like the old one.
And what is the first thing Crampton does?
He pulls himself together after the agreeable
shock, yields to the prompting of his heart, and
ferrets out with feverish haste his beloved gin
bottle from its familiar hiding place — if the
actor whom I saw in the part interpreted him
aright.[1] Naïve people have wondered why just
at the end Crampton should cap his fatherly
blessing with an anticlimax by calling young
Strähler a blockhead. Probably in his good
nature he pities the luckless husband who is
saddling himself with such a precious specimen
of a father-in-law. The drama "Colleague Crampton" suffers from an incurable weakness, the
absolute lack of character in its hero. And like
its predecessors it is again without a definitive
conclusion so far as it deals with Crampton's fate,
because no rational person will be optimistic
enough to believe in the permanent reform of
the old backslider.

[1] This "business," however, is not indicated in the text of the
play.

The next of Hauptmann's works in order of publication is *Der Biberpelz* (" The Beaver Coat") (1893), a naturalistic comedy of provincial life. Inasmuch, however, as it is linked together with *Der rote Hahn* (1901) by a sort of personal union, through the identity of the principal characters, we shall postpone its consideration for the present and turn our attention to another play.

With *Hannele* (1893) Hauptmann planted his feet on a different ground from that which he had hitherto stood on. Had he not reverted to naturalism after " The Sunken Bell," we might regard *Hannele* as the bridge that spans the gulf between his two widely separated phases of artistic creation. That even so this imaginative play betokens an experimental departure from absolute realism is seen at first glance in the outward form, in the shifting from prose to verse, and back again. Who would have expected a concession like that from the associate of Holz and Schlaf, from a dramatist who hitherto had felt obliged utterly to scorn rime, monologue, and many other recognized technical contrivances! And yet one ought to be prepared for abrupt changes in a poet whose fundamental mood results from the commixture of radical and reactionary tendencies, and has much in common with the cloudy world-conception of the Romantics of old, — a poet, moreover, by no means free from vanity, who seems to be incessantly aiming to surprise the world and chain criticism to his triumphal car. Hauptmann willingly lets himself be swept along with the tide of popular sentiment, but feeling himself, justly, a Triton among the minnows, he loves to swim in the lead.

I have already stated that in the realm of the fairy tale lies the sole territory of which Hauptmann is lord. Unquestionably, the poet himself never realized this limitation. And it may even be that he would never have exercised his genius in that field had not the *Märchendrama* just then enjoyed growing favor as a dramatic specialty; witness the phenomenal success of Fulda's Orientally costumed *Der Talisman* (1893), the homely opera *Hänsel und Gretel* (text by Adelheid Wette, music by E. Humperdinck), and other similar works of legend origin. It is not accidental that the commingling of naturalism and fantastic idealism is brought about in *Hannele* through the poetic device of a dream. That form of all others lends itself most readily to the bold experiment, for the dramatic reproduction of a dream does not presuppose strict causality and sequence. As every dream is woven of reality and imagination, it thus affords a sort of neutral territory for two forces which are apparently antagonistic in the contemporary practice of art. In the *Märchendrama* of earlier periods, notably in the efforts of its great masters Raimund and Grillparzer, the dream serves to introduce romantic situations which may be resolved at a moment's notice to give place to the actualities of real life. The contrivance is simple enough : at the critical moment the hero is made to return to waking consciousness. But while the trance lasts the poet has a fine opportunity to expose the intimate soul-life of his characters. Usually an allegoric or didactic purpose is conveyed; so in Raimund, Grillparzer, and Fulda.

By the form chosen, the harsh contrasts presented in *Hannele* — its alternation of prose and verse, vulgar dialect and cultivated speech, its constant clash between the squalor of the *milieu* and the glorious forms shaped by the poet's vaulting imagination — are excused or at least extenuated. We view with easy tolerance the

bold adversative of poorhouse and heaven, pau-
pers and angels, of sweet, pious Hannele and the
village slattern Hete. The dramatic presupposi-
tions are arbitrary, inconsistent, and impossible.
It is intended that the entire action should be
tangible and each personality stand out con-
cretely; for this the author depends, as usual, to
an unreasonable degree on the make-up of the
characters.[1]

On the other hand, the center of interest is
translated from the actual to a world of appari-
tions, and the most powerful imagination of the
audience is put into commission to picture Hannele lying fatally ill in bed and at the same time
taking part in a *commedia dell' arte* born of her
feverish visions.

To account for the astonishing success of
Hannele, — at first the play bore the title *Hannele's Himmelfahrt* ("The Assumption of Hannele") — it is only necessary to read it in an
unprejudiced frame of mind. From every line
of it pours forth that rich stream of purest
human sympathy, which, flowing from a true

[1] Here is an example: "Enter Magistrate Berger, a *Captain* of the
Reserves, as no one can fail to notice." Is such a stage direction anything short of unconscious comicality, in view of the fact that the
magistrate is in civilian clothes?

poet-soul, bubbles up irresistibly even through
the naturalistic rubbish of the earlier works.

The plot in *Hannele* is almost as lean and
somber as in the former efforts of Hauptmann.
In his drunken rage a ruffianly stepfather so
maltreats his fourteen-year-old daughter that she
seeks refuge in death and throws herself into the
water. She is pulled out by kindly people and
carried to the poorhouse for nursing. Here the
village schoolmaster, a deaconess, the country
doctor, the magistrate, even several inmates of
the poorhouse, take loving care of the unfortunate child. But she is past human help. Her
terrible agitation and the fever have between
them irreparably shattered her frail little body.
Delirium colors things and people with the hues
of her childish fantasy. The poet with exquisite touch ushers us into the atmosphere of dream-
land. In the dream action the characters are none
other than the persons of the sick-room trans-
figured by the imagination of the little sufferer.
Her desperate act, too, is thus glorified, for she
is under the delusion that Jesus himself invited
her into the water. All that passes is unreal,
and yet in the fantastic action how much of
Hannele's soul is revealed! We descend to the

depths of her subconscious being, just as by a
different process we are led to know the un-
guarded souls of the mad Ophelia and Gretchen.
The poet has succeeded in making Hannele's
hallucinations entirely vivid to the reader, notably when he conjures up before her eyes the
terrifying appearance of her bestial stepfather.
And at the same time his adequate art has
penciled with discreetly delicate lines the first
dawning love experience of the ripening young
girl. To attain such truly poetic results Hauptmann had to rise subjectively above his crude
material. Therein lies the significance of *Hannele* for his art-practice. The naturalists have
often proclaimed their self-satisfied belief that
it is far more difficult to objectify a transverse
section of real life from without than to build
up its semblance from the inner consciousness.
In *Hannele* Hauptmann undertakes to expose to
view a transverse section, as it were, of a human
soul. He makes a practical attempt at psychology. Certainly this is an infinitely difficult and
delicate task, and one which in the present instance could be accomplished only with the assist-
ance of old and well-tried dramatic expedients.
But he has not discarded the modern technical

acquisitions, either. *Hannele*, in fact, represents the application of modern technic to an all but obsolete variety of the drama. Or is it other than melodramatic when we see shadowy forms flit, to the strains of soft music, across the simple soul of the little martyr who languishes in rags on her bed of straw, while fever dreams delude her with the fabulous splendor of her celestial reward?

Hannele is a melodrama, even in the current meaning of the word, i.e. an *Ausstattungsstück*. We see with wonder the stout disciple of Bjarne Holmsen throwing himself into the circles of the spectacular play. The elaborate allegorical apparatus readily calls to mind the second part of *Faust* and Ferdinand Raimund's magic pieces. But more than these plays *Hannele* is instinct with genuine human pathos.

True it is, as has been pointed out, that the component elements of the play are at variance with one another, yet in the effect produced by *Hannele* as a whole the outer visible misery is only subservient to the touching portrayal of Hannele's martyrdom and deliverance. The naturalistic part of *Hannele* is decidedly secondary in importance to the idealistic.

The technical treatment of the desolate environment against which the idealized figure of Hannele stands out in shining relief is fully in accord with the method employed in " Before Sunrise" and " The Weavers." In the higher sphere Hauptmann's genius bursts the somber chrysalis and, spreading its brilliant wings, soars high above the arid sobriety of the actual. Who would have suspected so much splendor of rhythm and color in the author of " The Weavers "? Listen to the entrancing " Song of the Stranger ":

THE SONG OF THE STRANGER [1]

The City of the Blessèd is marvellously fair,
And peace and utter happiness are never-ending there.
The houses are of marble, the roofs of gold so fine,
And down their silver channels bubble brooks of ruby wine.
The streets that shine so white, so white, are all bestrewn with
    flowers,
And endless peals of wedding bells ring out from all the towers.
The pinnacles, as green as May, gleam in the morning light,
Beset with flickering butterflies, with rose-wreaths decked and
    dight.
Twelve milk-white swans fly round them in mazy circles wide,
And preen themselves, and ruffle up their plumage in their pride ;

[1] The translation is from the English version of the play by W. Archer (Heinemann, London, 1898).

They soar aloft so bravely through the shining heavenly air,
With fragrance all a-quiver and with golden trumpet-blare ;
In circle-sweeps majestical forever they are winging,
And the pulsing of their pinions is like harp-strings softly ringing.
They look abroad o'er Sion, on garden and on sea,
And green and filmy streamers behind them flutter free —
And underneath them wander, throughout the heavenly land,
The people in their feast-array, forever hand in hand ;
And then into the wide, wide sea, filled with the red, red wine,
Behold ! they plunge their bodies with glory all a-shine —
They plunge their shining bodies into the gleaming sea,
Till in the deep clear purple they 're swallowed utterly ;
And when again they leap aloft rejoicing from the flood,
Their sins have all been washed away in Jesus' blessèd blood.

In *Hannele* we have seen that Hauptmann takes himself out of the file of the intransigent naturalists. It was Karl Gutzkow who once said, " Every true poet becomes a symbolist, but for the poet of masculine temperament history provides the guise." That is to say, for the aspirations of such a poet the historical drama supplies the fittest vehicle of expression. Now it has been stated of Hauptmann, without any disparagement of his high poetic virtues, that he is not properly a poet of the masculine type. For this reason his experiment in historical drama miscarried.

The historical drama, more than any other form of literary production, demands on the part of its author the exercise of hard, uncompromising logic and a keen historical sense; both are beyond Hauptmann's capacity. Karl Bleibtreu hits the point exactly when he finds in Hauptmann's *Florian Geyer* only the outer garb of an epoch, not its flesh and sinew.

With the first representation on the stage of his one historical play (January 4, 1896) our poet experienced his first and only complete failure.[1] From the effects of this blow it is said he has never been able to recover. I believe that Hauptmann's severance from extreme naturalism was indirectly responsible for this fiasco. While still under the spell of that doctrine the poet had undertaken with might and main the great experiment foreshadowed in " The Weavers " of applying the so-called scientific method to a strictly historical subject. He may have anticipated for his work the same explosive effect that was produced in the eighteenth century by Goethe's *Götz von Berlichingen*. During the execution of

---

[1] Very recently the play, in an abridged and somewhat altered form, has been staged again; at the present writing it is being given with fair success in Berlin.

the project, however, he had begun to recover from naturalism in its acutest form. It is extremely difficult for an artist under the circumstances either to throw away his work or to recast it. The original notions with obsessive force determine its form. So Hauptmann worked on with broken purpose and laboriously completed the work in the same manner in which it was begun ; the result satisfied neither the old standard nor the new.

The historic Florian Geyer,[1] who resembles in many points the Knight of Berlichingen, was the ablest and most loyal leader of the insurgents. Had it been Sudermann who handled this theme he would undoubtedly have found the tragedy to consist in the fact that Geyer, who though a noble by birth forsakes his hereditary sphere to champion the rights of the seditious peasants and stand sponsor for their most radical demands, is repudiated by both factions and cruelly hounded to death because he holds right and justice higher than party allegiance. This tragedy of the *déclassé* Hauptmann barely indicates. The leader of the " Black Band " falls out with his mercenary fellow rebels and cannot outlive the wreck

---

[1] See Bensen's *History of the Peasant War in East Franconia in 1525.*

of the ideals he has defended. For the rest
Hauptmann is content to paint in broad diorama
a succession of impressionistic pictures of the long
ago, joined together after a fashion, yet not sum-
ming up, somehow, to a full-orbed dramatic action.
So far as we are informed through the play alone
the end is too much like an unfortunate accident.
A true dramatist must be able to persuade us that
the end could not possibly have been otherwise.[1]
Another fault of this much too long tragedy is
that it lacks an orderly arrangement. The chaotic
action is disconcerting and disturbs the compo-
sure indispensable for æsthetic enjoyment. The
historic background is woven in with undeniable
skill, but in the end one loses the thread in the
maze of details. Finally the diction, for which
Hauptmann had so diligently scoured the old
chronicles, is a stumbling-block for a modern
audience. Without at all impugning its accuracy,
how much has been actually gained for the
realism of the play when the result of repristina-
tion is to make the utterance sound strange and
harsh to all but to the German philologian?

[1] The drama should be the place where we may see, more easily
recognizable than in actual life, the universal operation and validity of
irresistible law. — E. WOODBRIDGE, *The Drama, its Law and its Tech-
nique*, p. 44.

In one respect *Florian Geyer* resembles " The Weavers." In Hauptmann's hands Florian is not the real hero, holding the dramatic interest from beginning to end. The principal rôle is played by the singular uprising of one whole social estate against another, or if one looks for something at least more concrete, " Poor Conrad," the rebellious peasantry, is the surrogate hero, just as the starving proletariat was in " The Weavers." But the greater dramatic weakness of the newer play comes to light in the fact that the poet is silent as to the cause of the uprising. The rebel peasants of the rank and file do not appear until the fifth act, so that we are not directly moved to pity by their lot; possibly Hauptmann takes it for granted that we remember all about their woes from our high-school days. The cast, by the way, comprises no fewer than sixty-one persons.

Geyer does not stand out in bold relief against the large and confused living background as does Shakespeare's Julius Cæsar or Coriolanus. The attempt to characterize each of so many figures detracts from his due importance as the central figure. Hauptmann is not enough of a dramatist to have succeeded in an indirect characterization of his hero, such as Schiller gives when he prepares us so happily for the domineering figure of Wallenstein by picturing the spirit that rules in his camp, explaining thus, even before the commander appears, his transgression and downfall through his forceful, dangerful influence over the masses.

These various failings effectually blocked for *Florian Geyer* the way to public favor at a time when amid the exultant joy that greeted Wildenbruch's trilogy *Heinrich und Heinrichs Geschlecht* ("King Henry and his House") (1896) it seemed as if ultra-naturalism were now to be marched out of the theater to the familiar beat of Schiller's iambic pathos.

Hauptmann misconstrued the symptomatic significance of this defeat, which was a censure less for the man than for the school by which, after all, he stood with but partial allegiance. His sicklied imagination exaggerated the meaning of his failure, as though he had staked all his power on a great undertaking and had found to his utter dismay that his strength was inadequate.

Out of his ungrounded despondency sprang the germ of a new poem calculated to allay his self-distrust: an allegoric work which, far outstripping anything he had previously performed, insured

for many years, perhaps forever, an honorable
place for his name among those who by satisfying the best judges of their own time deserve to
live for all ages.

Denn wer den Besten seiner Zeit genug
Getan, der hat gelebt für alle Zeiten.

"The Sunken Bell" is just as little a drama
as *Hannele*, perhaps even less so, but nevertheless it is an art work of singular beauty, couched
in language of a poetic splendor unparalleled in
modern letters and fraught with a pure and truly
German inwardness. The real worth of this poem
does not lie in its far-sought symbolism, but in the
wondrous atmosphere suffusing the whole and
transporting us by its magic into the heart of
the old romantic land of Tieck, Eichendorff, and
Fouqué, where the brooks babble and the trees
whisper and the winds make music to it all. In
this fantastic world Gerhart Hauptmann fairly
revels, combining in his all-perceptive sense for
the beauties and mysteries of nature the eye of a
Böcklin with the ear of a Mendelssohn-Bartholdy.
Never yet has a poet stood in a more intimate
sensuous relation to nature; at least no poet has
been more successful in vivifying her.

Out of the well among the soughing pines, spluttering and blinking, the Nickelmann (water sprite) pulls himself up, annoyed at first by the unaccustomed glare of the spring sunshine. From the thicket the wood sprite capers into the clearing, a comical, carnal-minded fellow, goat footed, horned, and whiskered, pipe in mouth, a swarm of flies buzzing round him. He has broken away for a while from the humdrummery of domestic life, for a change from the boresome Missus and her nine dirty little brats, and now drinks in contentedly the joy of May-time. The smell of springtide is in the air, as Rautendelein reminds the Nickelmann:

> Ay, ay —
> It smells of springtide. Well, is that so strange?
> Why, every lizard, mole, and worm, and mouse —
> The veriest water-rat — had scented that.
> The quail, the hare, the trout, the fly, the weeds,
> Had told thee spring was here —

What a fascinating familiarity with the nocturnal gambols of the elfin folk is felt in the charming roundelay! [1]

---

[1] The passages from "The Sunken Bell" are quoted from the excellent translation of the play by Charles Henry Meltzer (Doubleday & McClure Company, New York, 1901).

First Elf (whispering)

Sister !

Second Elf (as above)

Sister !

First Elf (as above)

White and chill
Shines the moon across the hill.
Over bank and over brae,
Queen she is and queen shall stay.

Second Elf

Whence com'st thou?

First Elf

From where the light
In the waterfall gleams bright,
Where the glowing flood doth leap
Roaring down into the deep.
Then, from out the mirk and mist,
Where the foaming torrent hissed,
Past the dripping rocks and spray,
Up I swiftly made my way.

Third Elf (joining them)

Sisters, is it here ye dance?

First Elf

Wouldst thou join us?   Quick — advance !

Second Elf

And whence com'st thou?

Third Elf

Hark and hist !
Dance and dance, as ye may list !

'Mid the rocky peaks forlorn
Lies the lake where I was born.
Starry gems are mirrored clear
On the face of that dark mere.
Ere the fickle moon could wane,
Up I swept my silver train.
Where the mountain breezes sigh,
Over clove and crag came I.

Fourth Elf (entering)

Sisters !

First Elf

Sister ! Join the round !

All (together)

Ring-a-ring-a-ring-around !

Fourth Elf

From Dame Holle's flowery brae,
Secretly I stole away.

First Elf

Wind and wander, in and out.

All (together)

Ring-a-ring-a-round-about !

(Lightning and distant thunder.)

(Enter suddenly, from the hut, Rautendelein. Clasping her hands behind her head,
she watches the dance from the doorway. The moonlight falls full on her.)

Rautendelein

Ho, my fairies !

First Elf

Hark ! A cry !

Second Elf

Owch !   My dress is all awry !

Rautendelein

Ho, ye fairies !

Third Elf

Oh, my gown !

Flit and flutter, up and down.

Rautendelein (joining in the dance)

Let me join the merry round,
Ring-a-ring-a-ring-around !
Silver nixie, sweetest maid,
See how richly I 'm arrayed.
All of silver, white and rare,
Granny wove my dress so fair.
Thou, my fairy, brown, I vow
Browner far am I than thou.
And, my golden sister fair,
I can match thee with my hair.
Now I toss it high — behold,
Thou hast surely no such gold.
Now it tumbles o'er my face :
Who can rival me in grace?

All (together)

Wind and wander, in and out,
Ring-a-ring-a-round-about !

Hauptmann's genius has power to gift with
life from the welling spring of his own rich artist
soul all the elemental forces of nature. In " The

Sunken Bell" whatever moves, lives. Hear the
spell spoken by Rautendelein as she bustles about
the hearth over her work as sick-nurse:

> Flickering spark in the ash of death,
> Glow with life of living breath!
> Red, red wind, thy loudest blow!
> I, as thou, did lawless grow!
> Simmer, sing, and simmer!
>
> *(The flame leaps up on the hearth.)*
>
> Kettle swaying left and right—
> Copper-lid, thou 'rt none too light!
> Bubble, bubble, broth and brew,
> Turning all things old to new!
> Simmer, sing, and simmer!
>
> Green and tender herbs of spring
> In the healing draught I fling.
> Drink it sweet, and drink it hot—
> Life and youth are in the pot!
> Simmer, sing, and simmer!

Just as long as Hauptmann symbolically vivi-
fies nature his poetry pours forth with a spontaneous and irresistible charm. "The Sunken Bell"
is instinct with an all-embracing nature-sense;
nearly the whole gamut of nature's varying moods
is run, from the awful to the idyllic. But as soon
as he oversteps his limitations and tries through

the symbol to give concrete shape to the unsub-
stantial, the forces that rule within or above in-
sentient nature, he finds them inconvertible and
quickly loses himself in subtilties. To submit just
one example, it is decidedly farfetched when at
the beginning of the fourth act the six talents
involved in the creation of a poetical work, to wit:
Intellect, Energy, Inspiration, Indecision, Self-
Criticism, and Self-Discipline, are personified as
six dwarfs forced into servitude by the bell founder
Heinrich. By a Goethe growing old and whim-
sical we meekly allow ourselves to be mystified;
but even from such a Goethe to Hauptmann it is
a far cry.

"The Sunken Bell" has appeared in an almost
unprecedented number of editions in the original
text, and it has been turned several times into
English; of these translations that of Mr. Meltzer
is, in my opinion, the one in spirit most allied to
the original. The play has been performed in this
country by German actors, including that ideal
Rautendelein, Agnes Sorma, and it has been produced also under American management, with a
cast to be sure which failed to catch the elfin
airiness of the piece. At any rate, the story is
so well known — even "Mr. Dooley" has made

capital out of it — that we may save ourselves
the ungrateful task of turning at length so exquisitely dainty a composition into barren prose.
About its symbolic meaning, however, something
must be said.

The story, briefly retold, runs thus: A bell,
intended to proclaim afar the praise of the Creator and the fame of its maker, falls down a steep
bank and is lost in the mountain lake. The
maker, heartsick because he has discovered that
the bell is not the masterpiece it is thought to
be by all the people, throws himself after his
handiwork.

> I fell. I know not how — I've told thee that —
> Whether the path gave way beneath my feet,
> Whether 't was willingly I fell, or no —
> God wot. Enough. I fell into the gulf.

But he does not perish. Half dead from the fall,
he drags himself to a lonely hut. Here lives
Granny Wittichen, a notorious witch, together
with an elfin creature, the golden-haired Rautendelein. With this girl, who is conceived as a
personification of nature, Master Heinrich falls in
love, and forsakes wife and children to dwell
with her in the mountain wilds. There he sets

up his workshop. Among the great, free heights,
with soul raised aloft by fresh incentive, he feels
the access of new power to accomplish that which
was denied him in the spiritual solitude down in
the valley: he will work up into form a wondrous
chime, —

> Such as no minster in the world has seen.
> Loud and majestic is its mighty voice;
> Even as the thunders of a storm it sounds,
> Rolling and crashing o'er the meads in spring.
> Ay, in the tumult of its trumpet tones,
> All the church bells on earth it shall strike dumb.
> All shall be hushed, as through the sky it rings
> The glad new Gospel of the new-born light!

On this new gospel — a symbolic sun worship
that shall absorb and humanize our religion — he
addresses an ecstatic harangue to the vicar, who
has come to reclaim Heinrich for his abandoned
duty.

> Eternal Sun! Thy children and my children
> Know thee for Father and proclaim thy power.
> Thou, aided by the kind and gentle rain,
> Didst raise them from the dust and give them health!
> So now their joy triumphant they shall send
> Singing along thy clear, bright path to Heaven!
> And now, at last, like the gray wilderness
> That thou hast warmed, and mantled with thy green,

Me thou hast kindled into sacrifice !
I offer thee myself, and all I am ! . . .
O Day of Light — when from the marble halls
Of my fair Temple the first waking peal
Shall shake the skies — when, from the somber clouds
That weighed upon us through the winter night,
Rivers of jewels shall go rushing down
Into a million hands outstretched to clutch !
Then all who drooped, with sudden power inflamed,
Shall bear their treasure homewards to their huts,
There to unfurl, at last, the silken banners,
Waiting — so long, so long — to be upraised,
And, pilgrims of the Sun, draw near the feast !

.   .   .   .

O Father, that great Day ! . . . You know the tale
Of the lost Prodigal? . . . It is the Sun
That bids his poor, lost children to the Feast.
With rustling banners, see the swelling host
Draw nearer, and still nearer to my Temple !
And now the wondrous chime again rings out,
Filling the air with such sweet, passionate sound
As makes each breast to sob with rapturous pain.
It sings a song, long lost and long forgotten,
A song of home — a childlike song of Love,
Born in the waters of some fairy well —
Known to all mortals, and yet heard of none !
And as it rises, softly first, and low,
The nightingale and dove seem singing, too,
And all the ice in every human breast

Is melted, and the hate, and pain, and woe,
Stream out in tears.

.   .   .   .

Then shall we all draw nearer to the Cross,
And, still in tears, rejoice, until at last
The dead Redeemer, by the Sun set free,
His prisoned limbs shall stir from their long sleep,
And, radiant with the joy of endless youth,
Come down, himself a youth, into the May.

But Heinrich's fair dream is not realized, because
he has not left his human conscience behind him
in the valley. His faithlessness drives his loyal
wife to suicide, — for Hauptmann's characters the
natural escape from sorrow; a vision shows him
his little children toiling up towards him with a
jug containing the dead mother's tears. Master
Heinrich's soul is harrowed by remorse; the man
in him is broken, and with that the artist goes to
pieces also. The sunken bell, touched by the dead
wife's fingers, tolls a loud warning. Heinrich,
wholly beside himself, curses and spurns poor
Rautendelein, but soon discovers that he cannot
do without her. To the life of the valley he cannot return; his forest temple goes up in flames.
And so, without a home on the shining heights,
without a home in the netherland, he must die.

That "The Sunken Bell" is the work of a real, whole-souled poet is certified by every line. A rare poetic temperament pulsates through every fiber of the whole composition. Poetically "The Sunken Bell" can hardly be praised too much. Its situations and characters are so entrancing, the language is so beautiful, that we may draw pure delight from each constituent part, even though we may not understand the allegory that is hidden in it.

As for the underlying tissue of personal experience, it is but thinly veiled. Yet a great many have enjoyed "The Sunken Bell" without going to the trouble of tracing out the resemblance of Master Heinrich the bell-founder to Master Gerhart the playwright. Nothing could better argue the intrinsic poetical value of the work.

We have so far spoken of "The Sunken Bell" as a poem, as a lyric effusion cast in dialogue, if such a description is admissible. Our praise cannot be equally unstinted when we view "The Sunken Bell" as a drama and a channel of philosophic thought. It is then that we miss, back of the lovely allegory, the clarified world-view of a ripened individuality. And such we have been taught by our great dramatists to expect.

The tragic fate of Master Heinrich would infallibly have appealed to us had the poet fully convinced us of his hero's overmanship. In that case Master Heinrich might have been reckoned among those brethren-in-fate of Faust whom we hesitate to judge according to the usual standards of human conduct. As it is, he is too small of stature to be compared with Faust, even though he does distantly resemble him. Faust triumphs because he *is* an overman, Heinrich perishes because he would like to be. He is a calamitous blend of the Titan's ambition and the weakling's lack of self-control, a hybrid between overman and decadent. His flight from the narrower circles of life looks suspiciously like an escapade. No lofty fellowship of spirit or congeniality of mind, no profound mutual comprehension joins Heinrich and Rautendelein by main force; nothing but a sensual attraction draws them together. And the sacred fires in Heinrich's new-built temple cannot long be kept glowing when fanned only by such a fickle breeze as his passion for Rautendelein. If the fate of Heinrich, the lesser mystic, fails to wring from us as much sympathy as we feel for the greater mystic, Faust, it is principally because we ourselves are more nearly concerned in the fate of Faust. The great problems of life which he finally solves in spite of all hindrances are of universal human relevancy. The whole aim and endeavor of Hauptmann's hero, on the other hand, is centered exclusively on artistic ideals, to realize which he deserts his nearest obligations. In spite of all its beauties "The Sunken Bell," after all, does not appeal irresistibly to all our human nature at once, because it deals with human nature under exceptional aspects.

The enthusiastic acceptance of "The Sunken Bell" served as an unmistakable sign of the trend of the literary taste. For the poet himself as well as for the public it testified to the truth of the blunt saying in Paul Heyse's anti-naturalistic novel *Merlin:* "Though with the pitchfork of naturalism we may drive out never so vigorously that longing for the great and beautiful which is called idealism, it forever returns."

In determining Hauptmann's position in modern letters, this poetic achievement has advanced essentially its author's reputation and won for him many who formerly were averse or skeptical. By no means, however, does it raise him to the rank of the *facile princeps* among

living poets; for it is a distinguishing characteristic of the German mind that the mere sensuous
beauty of an art work does not wholly satisfy it.
The Germans want to look up to their great
poets not only as to magicians who produce a
transient semblance of the beautiful, but also as
to teachers of wisdom and guides through the
wildernesses and labyrinths of life. All present
symptoms point strongly to the fact that they
demand that their dramatists draw characters
who, on the one hand, shall be perfectly true to
life, but who also, in addition to their transient
individual significance, shall have a universal,
profound, close human relationship with us and
thereby move us to such a personal participation
in their fate as no mere stranger ever can compel
on his own account. So far as we have made their
acquaintance, Hauptmann's heroes are either —
as Master Heinrich — symbols in human shape,
in which case they lack the requisite red-blooded
personality, or they are the superficial likenesses
of men who are caught with astounding accuracy
in their characteristics of attitude and speech, yet
are without a lasting interest because the inner-
most secret of their identity with ourselves is not
revealed.

After " The Sunken Bell " it seems as if our poet were conscious of the inadequacy of past efforts, and had at last found the road to a genuine realistic character drama. Certainly it can be only a hasty examination which finds in *Fuhrmann Henschel* (" Henschel the Teamster ") (1898) nothing but a relapse of the successful *Märchendichter* into reluctant fidelity to his old love, Naturalism. In *Florian Geyer* Hauptmann had essayed the application of naturalism to historic drama. In *Fuhrmann Henschel* another experiment is made, in which the naturalistic impressionism is employed as an aid to the true function of the drama now apparently conceived as the revealment of the psychology not of a social throng, as in *Die Weber* and in *Geyer*, but of an individual. The transition from a physiologic to a psychologic type of impressionism is thus distinctly marked; a progress which, as has been well pointed out by the historian Karl Lamprecht, is in line with the general trend of modern literary development. Already from the middle of the nineties Hauptmann's plays had ceased to be regarded by ultra-naturalists like Holz as patterns and paradigms of their theory. Perhaps now, in the retrospection, we can better understand the apparently saltatory progress of Hauptmann. That he had outgrown the obstructive ordinances of naturalism there can be no question. Yet he did not turn utter renegade, because he recognized the permanent gain accruing to the drama from the late reform; rather he sought to find a means by which, without sacrificing this gain, he might attain a less one-sided manifestation of his powers. In *Hannele*, as we have seen, the theme was chosen with singular felicity so as to permit the unmixed coexistence of the seamy and the dreamy worlds. In " The Sunken Bell " naturalism was pushed to the wall by the long-repressed *furor poeticus*. But Hauptmann is naturally unwilling to relinquish a method which furnishes the sole opportunity for one of the most potent elements in his genius, namely, his unexcelled power of observation and reproduction. The new peasant drama combines the physiological and the psychological methods. It retains all the external verisimilitude of "The Weavers," yet the interest is never, as there, focused on the environment, but on the *Auswicklung*, the unfolding of the central character.

Fuhrmann Henschel is a Silesian dialect drama, like *Die Weber*. The situations are very much like those in *Bahnwärter Thiel*. Henschel, a

rough, stupid, but well-meaning and deeply conscientious fellow, has solemnly promised his dying
wife (in act i) that he will not marry Hanne
Schäl, the house servant, of whom she is jealous.
Having for domestic reasons broken his promise
to the dead, the superstition preys on his mind
that he is gradually being forfeited to her revenge.
Meanwhile the wily, sensuous Hanne develops
into a reckless village Messalina. With hardened
villainy she practices one deception after another
upon her hulking, good-natured husband, robbing
him of his domestic happiness, his child, his honor,
his prestige, his substance, and thus finally of reason and of life itself. The end (which is suicide)
is thus brought on without the coöperation of
the tragic guilt of the hero, formerly held to be
one of the essentials of tragedy. In the story of
Fuhrmann Henschel the realistic method is not
employed with the unscrupulous thoroughness of
former plays, so that, among other things, all
ribaldry and nastiness are dispensed with; a single
obscenity occurs. It is true that, for the purpose
of making up a definite *milieu*, various supernu-
merary characters like Siebenhaar and Franziska
Wermelskirch wander detachedly about in this
play as in the earlier ones, but the figure of

Wilhelm Henschel is skillfully moved into the foreground and kept there throughout the five acts. Nevertheless, it must be acknowledged that Hauptmann has not fully risen above his limitations; for even Henschel's tragic fate seems painted al fresco and much of the psychological motiving is left to the onlooker. Besides, the plot is not fairly rounded out, since in the last act, when the will power of the hero is finally broken, the whole structure of the plot, unfinished as it is, collapses too, as though we had no interest in any one but Henschel. So much, however, we may regard as certain, without claiming an authoritative opinion, that this work of Hauptmann by the relative flawlessness of form and content marks a long stride forward in his artistic progress. At any rate, " Henschel the Teamster " must unquestionably be reckoned one of the greatest peasant tragedies ever written.

So numerous were the dramatizations of peasant life after *Fuhrmann Henschel* that it looked for a while as though the muse of the German drama were preparing to take up its permanent residence in the country. But she only wanted to recuperate from the strenuous exploitation of the metropolis; she was beginning to tire of the fad for the tragedy of artist life which was gradually becoming a somewhat monotonous form of literary endeavor; and she sought invigoration from the fostering soil. The *Heimatkunst* — vernacular art — thus came to be highly prized, and its popularity was soon in its turn encompassed by the peril of faddish over-specialization. Fortunately, however, literary specialization means the accretion of many facts hitherto unavailable for a writer and thereby eventually a visible widening of his horizon.

The real poet once he is recognized should feel himself raised above the temptation of following a fashionable specialty, be it for the sake of bread, be it for the still more meretricious reason of popularity. Hauptmann's later works, too, bear witness to his greater independence, to his plucky determination to advance to his goals along self-chosen paths. And yet in spite of his increasing freedom from technical bigotry, one cannot always help feeling that up to this time the picture of the dying swan on the title-page of "The Sunken Bell" carries an ominous significance hardly intended by the poet.

Certainly the tramp-comedy *Schluck und Jau* (1900) does not lay claim to any special weight or relative value among the works of Hauptmann.

If his first sustained effort, the rhapsodic *Prome-thidenlos*, savored strongly of Byron, *Schluck und Jau* is frankly reminiscent of the Induction to Shakespeare's *The Taming of the Shrew*. But whereas there the sport with Christopher Sly ends at the opening of the real play, in Hauptmann's *Spiel zu Scherz und Schimpf* ("Play in Joke and Jollity") the incident throughout clusters round two drunken vagabonds whom the Prince's jovial friend in a waggish mood has carried into the hunting lodge.

It is natural to think that Hauptmann purposed to take up the psychologic experiment just where Shakespeare left off, that he imagined the inward experience of a pauper who, awaking from a drunken stupor, finds himself through some miracle in the possession of princely wealth, rank, and power. However, his play moves less by psychologic forces than by the comicality of the ensuing deception of Jau, to which his comrade Schluck is forced to contribute by masquerading as his princely spouse. Jau readily accepts the explanation that his former squalid estate was only a temporary delusion from which he has just recovered, but amid his new magnificence remaining unchanged, a vulgar, crapulous glutton, he furnishes so much fun for his fancied "subjects" that the psychologic experiment is soon smothered in roaring comedy. Before long a pugnacious form of megalomania makes Jau unendurable and hastens the end of his glory. A sleeping-draught is administered and Jau removed to the lawn in front of the chateau where he was first picked up. His colleague Schluck has preceded him. In conclusion we are acquainted with the moral lesson of the play, which consists in a sententious truism about the inconstancy of fortune.

" The descendants of Alexander of Macedon became joiners and clerks in Rome. This bundle of patched homespun — but yesterday it paraded as a prince!" The prince and the pauper are equally strangers to the pomp and splendor through which they are ushered with different degrees of speed. The real value of a man is little more than that of Jau in his natural state. With such philosophy we are dismissed. It is not deep nor new, but the poet himself has warned us in the prologue not to take him too seriously:

> Und nehmt dies derbe Stücklein nicht für mehr,
> Als einer unbesorgten Laune Kind.

And we may account for the "crude little piece" by Richard M. Meyer's conjecture that

Hauptmann belongs to those poets with whom recreation itself is turned into poetical product.

In *Schluck und Jau* Hauptmann approaches real comedy more than in any other work. The play is indeed documentary evidence of a "happy, careless mood." Such moods, with Hauptmann, are excessively rare. But genuine humor we miss even in *Schluck und Jau*. For genuine humor is the medium of an optimistic view of life, a medium by which all things are gilded or sublimated. To this poet whom the gods have otherwise endowed so richly, that one divine gift seems to have been denied, because he is at bottom a pessimist through whose mind the world is refracted as a confused and wrangling mass. All his works — the comedies not excepted — betray this pessimistic world-view which in the last analysis appears to be concomitant with the lack of a higher intellectual potency.

If it is a fact that *Michael Kramer* (1900) was written to give the lie to critics like Richard M. Meyer, who had said of Hauptmann that he lacked "the higher intellect, the mastery in the realm of ideas, the power to deal with the abstract, the quick flash that lights up the mystery of things," he has only furnished his critics with an additional proof of their allegation.

In *Michael Kramer* (1900) the poet undertook a bold and thoroughly original task. In this play what is customarily regarded as the "action" is not worked out through the agency, nor even with the coöperation, of the real hero, — Michael Kramer is in no way the author of his son's tragic fate; such at least was the impression produced by the masterly *première* in Berlin. In fact the "action" is of a very indirect and subordinate importance; it serves merely as a psycho-dynamic means for drawing to the surface the inmost soul-life of the principal character, for carding out, as it were, his very heart and entrails. So far this is the most ambitious and possibly the most successful psychological study undertaken by Hauptmann.

Michael Kramer is the artist who just falls short of greatness, — a type nearly related to Master Heinrich and, less intimately, to Colleague Crampton, — a painter who has never won the prize of public favor because, on the one side, his high principles forbid him to prostitute his art, to debase it to unworthy purposes, and because, on the other side, his hand is no mate

for his inspiration, his brush no tool adequate to
his artistic purpose, so that Kramer's best powers
are hopelessly lost on that perplexing road that
leads from the first conception to the finished
work, and his best ideas never materialize on
the canvas. As Heinrich is the man of the bell
that is never to be cast, so is Kramer the man
of the picture forever unpainted; but here the
limit to a further comparison between the two
seems to be set, for Kramer's manfully conscious
persistence, even though it does not triumph, is a
far more creditable form of endeavor than Heinrich's hysterical chase after phantoms.

Kramer is concisely described by his daughter Michalina: " Father is terribly honest." As
Kramer belongs to the painters who heed not
Goethe's caution, *"Bilde Künstler, rede nicht!"*
— and has a pedagogue's habit of dwelling on his
convictions, we learn from his own lips that unlike
the moonstruck bell-founder he puts the main
stress on *duty:* " *der Mann muß Pflichten erken-
nen, hör'n Se.*" He invests this *maxima regula* of
his conduct with the emphasis of frequent reit-
eration. So he says to his disciple Lachmann:
" Always work, work, Lachmann. We 've got to
work, you know, Lachmann. Else we molder

alive. Just look at such a life, how such a man works, such a Böcklin. That leads to something, there's something to show for that. Not only what he paints; the whole fellow. Work, you know, is life, Lachmann."

Michael Kramer has been called sib to Master Heinrich and Colleague Crampton, but that the kinship is not very close has also been stated. True, he belongs to a type that has necessarily the greatest fascination for a man like Hauptmann, who is in love with his art, — desperately in love, as we sometimes say, or better, as we should always say, sacredly in love with it. He typifies the incompleted, fractional, or merely potential artist — *der unganze Künstler*, I should say in German. But this man's failure has lost its sting. A life long he has striven without winning the prize, yet his loyalty has been rewarded. That divine spark which alone can engender the truly great in art is missing from his breast; but for the lack he is compensated by the stirrings of a serious and sober idealism. He is an unswerving advocate of the Joy of Working, and that makes him a great teacher. Whoever comes to him as a willing pupil is mysteriously transformed. " As a beggarly little fellow he arrives," says Lachmann, "and then suddenly receives the accolade."

It is clear that the tragic pathos in Kramer's fate cannot be grounded in his misfortune that as an artist he does not come up to his ideals. We have to look for it somewhere else. That *summum bonum* of the artist — natural genius — which the parent lacks, was given to the lucky child. If the son became the fulfillment of the father, then all was well. "Not I, — thought I to myself, — but you, you perhaps." Or, quite at the end, "I was the husk; there lies the kernel." And now having to see how the lazy rascal seals his conscience hermetically against father, mother, sister, and against every protest of his own artist nature, miserably frittering away his genius as a common pothouse loafer, is not the cruel shame of it enough to eat away the father's heart? That, then, is his tragedy. Not enough that fate has twice forced Michael Kramer to lay his artist's ambition in the grave; he must also say of the human being which is the dearest to him in the world, the dearest because Michael bows before his son's full-orbed genius as though it were the noblest part of his own self: "There is n't a good fiber in him. The boy is worm-eaten at the core.

A bad fellow. A low fellow." The history of art teaches that by some odd perversity genius sometimes travels in the same yoke with moral turpitude. Benvenuto Cellini was as eminent a blackguard and desperado as he was a carver and chaser; Master Veit Stoss was a notorious forger, branded as such by the public executioner. Yet though the secrets of the "split personality" of those men are not of necessary concern for us, we do expect some explanation for the natural wickedness of a leading character in a modern play of the realistic-psychological sort. Knowing that the author is fully informed regarding the provenience of his people and the ætiology of their physical and mental conditions, we confidently turn to him for enlightenment; but before the enigma of Arnold Kramer's character the most discerning reader stands in utter perplexity.

Morally he resembles in no respect either of his parents. His physical ugliness — he has inherited from his father a lean, lanky frame, lopsided shoulders, and a slightly humped back — might, at a pinch, account for Arnold's crabbedness; it offers no fit explanation for his boundless depravity. Possibly Hauptmann felt that under the circumstances he owed it to his hearers to describe this

freak of nature all the more minutely; he has
decidedly overdone the thing, and yet it cannot
be said that we learn more and more of young
Kramer's character as the play progresses. In the
first act, in his behavior towards his mother, he
shows himself a brazen-faced, cowardly liar. The
second act unrolls the character portrait of the
father; no new light is shed on the extant picture
of the son. And his physiognomy is so fixed that
the third act, too, does not in any essential way
alter its aspect. Nay, even when in the last act
we see him safely coffined and hear the touching
obituary delivered by the agonized father, we
are in danger of forgetting the *de mortuis nil
nisi bonum.* For Arnold Kramer is to the bitter
end an incorrigible profligate; and the most that
could be said in his favor would be in the nature
of the cow-boy's epitaph, "He was a mighty bad
fellow in some ways, but then — he was worse in
others." In lieu of a real dramatic plot, a thin
thread of incident binds together in the four
acts of *Michael Kramer* the final chapter in
the wasted life of Kramer junior. Arnold is
enamored of a wayward damsel, who will none
of him. Exasperated beyond endurance by a
lucky rival, he threatens the latter's life. The

revolver is snatched from his hand; then Arnold
runs away and drowns himself. When all is said,
the unfortunate fact remains that young Kramer
is the weirdly true representative of a species of
degenerates who "happen" in well-regulated, nay
by some irony of fate even in the "best" families.
But I doubt sincerely whether the best possible
performance of this play — and I believe I have
seen just that — helps us to a deeper understanding of the type.

Architecturally *Michael Kramer* relapses from
the greater structural consistency of *Fuhrmann
Henschel*. The action is pushed forward jerkily
over the insipid first act to the most telling part of
the play; then after the appalling interview between father and son in which the second act ends,
it sinks to the level of hopeless banality in the
third act. With Arnold out of the way, a higher
plane is reached in the fourth act, which is cast in
a sort of disguised soliloquy. Lachmann is present on the scene, but plays no more active part
than the interlocutor in a minstrel troupe. The
thoughts uttered by Michael have a powerful,
human charm, without, however, being either very
new or remarkably profound. Wealth of ideas is
certainly not a strong point of Hauptmann's art.

From this opinion we are not converted by the "thieves-comedy" *Der Biberpelz* ("The Beaver Coat") (1893) and its sequel or, better, companion piece, *Der rote Hahn* ("The Red Cock") (1901), both strict *milieu* plays and, therefore, somewhat in the same relation to *Schluck und Jau* as, say *Die Weber* to *Hannele*. Remarkable in both, particularly in "The Beaver Coat," is the sure seizure of the externals. The atmosphere of a particular locality, situated this time not in the author's home district but "somewhere in the vicinity of Berlin," is reproduced with a startling fidelity. Given such a performance as that in the Deutsches Theater at Berlin, where the intentions of the author are carried out under his personal supervision and with careful attention to the smallest detail, the illusion is well-nigh complete. *Der Biberpelz* has been compared by nearly all the critics to Heinrich von Kleist's *Der zerbrochene Krug*, one of the few great comedies of which the Germans may boast. I confess that beyond the fact that in both plays the plot is enacted in a court room, I can see no good reason for drawing an analogy. The character of the judge in both cases deviates widely from the accepted pattern, but Kleist's Judge Adam is an old rake and

arrant knave, a veritable stage villain, whereas
Amtsvorsteher von Wehrhahn measures up to a
fair enough moral standard. Moreover, in the
older comedy the judge is the central figure, which
is not the case in the newer. That distinction
belongs to the washerwoman Wolff, a most interesting, double-dyed malefactress who commits her
villainies under the very nose of the incredibly
stupid magistrate and even gathers in official com-
mendation from that innocent. Wehrhahn, though
he occupies the second place, is drawn with infi-
nite care, and while the remaining ten persons are
only subsidiary, tireless and most successful labor
has been spent on their characterization also; they
all seem drawn direct from living models.

The action this time is rather more involute
than we are accustomed to find it in Hauptmann's
work, because the plot consists in a game of hide
and seek. Still, of a story there is not much to
tell. In the year 1887, during the *Septennats-
kampf* which turned on the peace strength of the
army, the new *Amtsvorsteher*, or district judge,
devotes the greater part of his energies to ferreting
out and harassing those "internal enemies" who
foment the war against the conserving forces of
the fatherland. He cultivates a keen scent for

political offenders, to the great detriment of his
efficiency as a magistrate. At this time a number
of crimes against property are committed in the
town. Frau Wolff, the chief culprit, in league
with poachers and "fences," conducts a thriving
business in contraband. One evening in company
with her husband she steals a cord of firewood
from the premises of a well-to-do citizen by the
name of Krüger. On the following day the victim
reports the theft, but Baron Wehrhahn does not
show very deep interest in the affair, for just then
he is on the trail of a case of leze majesty which
absorbs him much more than the affair in hand.
Krüger is not in his good books, anyway, as he
has the reputation of being a socialist. At the
present time he is in particularly bad odor on
account of a suspicious inmate of his house, a
Dr. Fleischer, who by the way is an absolutely
harmless scholar seeking rest and health in the
suburban quiet. The irascible old Krüger, whose
temper explodes under the overbearance and pry-
ing inquisitiveness of the magistrate, flares up
and roars out his anger at Baron Wehrhahn, the
Baron roars in return, and the thieves go scot free.
Later, Frau Wolff executes an order of her patron
Wulkow for Krüger's fur overcoat and pockets

the handsome fee of fifty-nine thalers for the
job. The third act in no way advances the action,
but is devoted almost wholly to character treatment. The character of Frau Wolff is lighted up
by a number of sympathetic touches, notably her
love of children and motherliness towards the
benevolent Dr. Fleischer. But her vicious traits
also come out more strongly than ever before, —
above all, her perfect art of dissimulation. Nothing
could appear more sincere than her indignation at
the light-fingered gentry, who should be cast out
neck and crop, she says, else "they 'll steal the
very roof from over one's head." The humor, we
see, is all in the situation, not in the characters
that are set off by it. A character like that of the
Wolff woman is too repugnant to elicit laughter
by itself. There is an analogy between the fourth
and the second acts strong enough to make the
play a little tedious towards the end in any render-
ing that is below the highest standard. In the
fourth act the sagacious Wehrhahn presides in
his office to receive information about the stolen
fur, but again his thoughts are preoccupied with
his imagined "sacred duty" to persecute with fire
and sword the enemies of state and society. Adolf
Bartels, the author of a book on Hauptmann, is

right in finding fault with Wehrhahn's incomprehensible stupidity. For one reason or another all parties needed for a full investigation are on the spot, — the plaintiff, the thief, the receiver of the stolen object, and an unimpeachable witness who has a clew to the whereabouts of the *corpus delicti*. The truth lies so close that this Prussian Solomon could not help rubbing his nose against it if he did not prefer to turn that useful organ aside and poke it into things that concern him not. The officialdom of modern Prussia is not free from its measure of human frailty; its most obvious fault is the *Strebertum*, that repulsive habit of keeping the eye peeled for the higher opportunity. This official toadyism Hauptmann undoubtedly meant to satirize in the figure of Wehrhahn, but he did so at too great a sacrifice of truth. Wehrhahn is not a sample of the Prussian police or judiciary, but its caricature. Anybody who has the slightest acquaintance with this highly efficient branch of the Prussian government will subscribe to Bartels' assertion that in a suburb of Berlin a blockhead like Wehrhahn could not hold his position for a single month; yet we find that gentleman in the undisturbed enjoyment of his emoluments a dozen years later.

Der rote Hahn (" The Red Cock ")[1] (1901) is labeled a " tragi-comedy in four acts." The German repertory was practically without any specimens of this class of play when Friedrich Hebbel wrote "A Tragedy in Sicily" (1845). In Hebbel's rather insignificant play the tragi-comic element hinges on the notion of the guardians of law and order themselves turning criminals and then conspiring to make an innocent man suffer the penalty for the foul murder which they have committed. Hauptmann, we have seen, was several times attracted by tragi-comic motives: " In *Schluck und Jau* the victim is first roughly handled by fate and then mocked into the bargain. In Colleague Crampton, who first incurs and next by a stroke of luck escapes the consequences of his folly, we have likewise a tragi-comic hero. In *Der Biberpelz* a tragi-comic spectacle was furnished by the systematic defeat of justice through its appointed preservers. Of this genus *Der rote Hahn* is another specimen. It furnishes a continuation to *Der Biberpelz*, or rather another series of scenes culled from the same precincts.

1 In German, *"jemandem den roten Hahn aufs Dach setzen"* means " to set a person's house on fire." The play in English might be named " The Fire Bugs."

Hauptmann in his infatuation with the principal characters of *Der Biberpelz* may have felt
that he had not yet done them full justice or
made the most of them. So he put them once
more into dramatic commission. True children
of Hauptmann that they are, time has wrought
no perceptible change in them. Von Wehrhahn
is still *Amtsvorsteher*, although his breast is now
adorned with a badge of distinction; he is the
same sturdy patriot as of old, still heart and
soul in high politics, and as hot as ever after the
social-democratic vermin. The admirable "Mutter
Wolffen," too, is still at her post, alert and active
in spite of her sixty years. Having buried her
first husband, she has joined her fortunes to those
of one Fielitz, who follows the double calling of a
shoemaker and a police spy. His latter employ-
ment accounts for the *entente cordiale* which Wehrhahn keeps up with the noble couple. The theme
and the groundwork of the tragi-comedy are the
same as in its preceding companion piece. Again
justice miscarries through the bungling political
zeal of the incompetent Wehrhahn and the arch-
knavery of Madame Wolff-Fielitz. While the
magisterial eye is riveted on *die höchsten Jüter
der Nation*, its falcon glances are withdrawn

from the criminal doings in the immediate surroundings. Several fires have occurred, and it is
an open secret that they have been laid by the
owners for the sake of the insurance money. On
the strength of a remark dropped by her son-in-
law regarding the value of the Fielitz property
as a site for a fine large house, Mother Fielitz
has made up her mind to have a little fire of
her own and works on and nags her faint-hearted
husband till he consents to aid and abet the
lucrative scheme. The couple contrive to be
away from home on the day when the fire breaks
out; the property is burnt to the ground (acts
i and ii). The third act passes in the official quar-
ters of Wehrhahn, who is in the act of examining
a number of witnesses with reference to the fire.
As usual his scent is sidetracked. The Fielitzes
have not the least difficulty in hoodwinking him,
and make him take up with eagerness the suggestion that the fire was the revenge of some political suspect against whom Fielitz had rendered
service. A stronger clew, however, points to an
imbecile lad whose father, although he happens
to be in a position to indicate the guilty persons,
is prevented by Wehrhahn from speaking his
mind; the proceedings in the court room resemble

strongly those in *Der Biberpelz*. Hauptmann is apparently as much in love with the anomalous situation as a painter who repeatedly treats the same object. In the fourth act Mother Fielitz has attained her purpose, the new house is under roof, and after the German custom the event is celebrated with the so-called *Richtschmaus*. Again the heroine is shown from a better, human side, as was the case in the third act of *Der Biberpelz*. By way of a quasi rational sanction of her conduct she is permitted to set forth at some length her pessimistic world-view. Her death from heart failure, however surprising it must be to her physician as well as to the audience, puts an effectual though abrupt stop to the vivid scenes which of themselves tend to no truly dramatic close.

The conclusions drawn from the earlier works of the famous Silesian that he lacks keen penetration and cannot contribute to the world's stock of ideas are in no wise shaken by his latest productions.

Der arme Heinrich (" Poor Heinrich ") (1902) deals with a German legend well known to English readers through " The Golden Legend " of Longfellow.

This time Hauptmann makes a vigorous attempt to expound in dramatic form the inner development of a human soul; but he succeeds only so far as he follows the lines laid down by his celebrated predecessor, Hartmann von Aue.

Hauptmann has chosen as a suitable vehicle of the romantic tale the iambic pentameter and has manifested in the somewhat conventional way, whereby the subject-matter is worked up in the five acts, a closer observance of the established routine. At first we find ourselves at the home of Gottfried, a tenant of the noble Count Heinrich von Aue. We make the acquaintance of the worthy farmer and his goodwife, and of their daughter Ottegebe, a girl just blooming into womanhood. Here Heinrich has decided to hide from the world the shameful malady with which, as a punishment for too great pride, he knows himself to be stricken. To the most loyal among his retainers, his kinsman Sir Hartmann von Aue,[1] Heinrich reveals his affliction in a scene of extraordinary dramatic power; Ottegebe has

---

[1] He is brought into the play by way of poetical tribute to the great mediæval epicist of that name who, in the beginning of the thirteenth century, wrote the novel in rimes entitled *Der arme Heinrich* upon which Hauptmann's work is based.

overheard him and, rushing forward in an ecstasy
in which religious fervor and earthly love are
insolubly welded, exclaims as she covers Heinrich's hands with frantic kisses:

> "Lord! my dear Lord! think of the Lamb divine!
> I know — I will it — I can bear the sins.
> I 've promised it! And thou shalt be redeemed."

The "little wife," so Ottegebe has formerly
been called in jest by Heinrich, has been told
that there lives a great surgeon at Salerno who
can cure lepers with the heart's blood of a pure
maiden. She now longs to sacrifice her life in
order that her beloved master may be freed from
his curse. In Heinrich, meanwhile, the will to
live wages a formidable combat with his manly
conscience. He has left human habitations and
lives like a brute in fields and woods. The hide-
ous ravages of the disease, added to his savage
neglect of his person, have made him terrible
and loathsome to behold. But Ottegebe, nothing
daunted, remains firm in her resolution. Spurned
and insulted by Heinrich, she falls into melancholy and physical decline. Her parents confide
her to the care of a pious hermit. Here Heinrich,
at last succumbing to the demoralizing effect of

his misery, seeks her out, ready to follow whither-
soever she lead.

Heinrich.   Maid, thou art mine !
Ottegebe.   I am the Lord's.   No, no.
          Woe me ! Ah come ! What say'st thou?
Heinrich.   For to me
          Is measured out but so much life, no more,
          As grants the hollow of thy blessèd hand.

The fifth act takes place in Heinrich's ancestral
castle, where preparations are made by Hartmann for a joyous reception. And now Heinrich
returns, himself again in mind and body. He
has been cured of the plague, not through the
vicarious self-immolation of Ottegebe, but, on the
contrary, just because in the supreme moment
he found it in him to rise above his love of self,
to prevent the sacrifice, and to accept his fate as
an immutable decree of Providence. With this
hard-earned submission to the power of God,
Heinrich — Hauptmann's as well as Hartmann's
— has won his deliverance from the judgment.
And the end, too, is the same in both versions.
Hartmann von Aue, in bold defiance of the strong
caste spirit which dominates in the literature of
the age of chivalry, marries Heinrich to his yeo-
man's daughter. In the play, also, the wedding

bells are sounded for the regenerate knight and
his virgin redeemer. The legendary character of
Ottegebe is not entirely preserved by Hauptmann. As in *Hannele*, he does not hesitate to
contaminate the young girl's saintliness with an
erotic element, and by a mystic touch each of the
conflicting emotions gains weight from the other.
It may be questioned whether the poet has done
wisely to superadd to the heavenly heroism and
the sentimental love a suggestion of incipient
sex-life. *Der arme Heinrich* has been called a
mystery play of love; but in order that Ottegebe's
pure soul should mirror forth, together with the
love of God, the saving grace of human affection,
it was hardly necessary that she should have
been depicted as a young flagellant vigorously
plying the scourge on her body to suppress
satanic temptations. True it is that Hauptmann
has been able perfectly to reconcile this premature manifestation of sensuality with absolute
modesty and saintly chastity. Nevertheless the
eternally-and-spiritually-feminine by which Heinrich von Aue was drawn onward to a saving
conversion did not require the admixture of
physiological motives. But it may be that it
has heightened the "secessionist" nimbus which

hovers round Ottegebe and a few other women in Hauptmann's plays, notably the Princess Sidsilill in *Schluck und Jau*.

Still another difference between the two versions deserves to be noted. In the Middle-High-German story the horrors of the *miselsuht* with which the hero is afflicted are nowhere described with vivid detail. It is enough that the misery to which Heinrich is reduced is contrasted in a general way with his rank and wealth. It remained for Gerhart Hauptmann, after the moderns had bodied forth on the stage with such great gusto a variety of inherited diseases, to present a true or, at any rate, a sickening stage-view of leprosy. So, as in *Hannele*, the crass realism of one portion of the play contrasts with the poetic romanticism of the other; the conflict seems far greater, as the metrical uniformity of the plan makes no allowance for the discrepancy and the work is pitched to a high average level of poetic dignity. Would not the author have done better to let us behold the physical misery of Heinrich through a veil, as it were, instead of outraging our sensibilities by uncalled-for explicitness? His occasional independence of naturalism has already been pointed out in this chapter; and in the present instance one is led to regret that Heinrich is not treated with as much reserve as Ottegebe. Although *Der arme Heinrich* contains many single passages aglow with wondrous poetic beauty, yet it is not, as a whole, up to the standard of Hauptmann's chief poetic efforts.

Hauptmann has named his latest five-act play, *Rose Bernd* (1903), a *Schauspiel;* a designation which under the customary classification pertains to a serious play with a tragic tendency but a non-fatal ending. The difference, if it could be applied to *Rose Bernd*, would be at most purely superficial. The name, in fact, does not signify.[1]

Rose Bernd is a tragedy in every sense except that the heroine is withdrawn from our view this side of her last extremity. Not that the author shrank from the issue. Were we to behold Rose the infanticide on her way to the place of execution, or were we harrowed by her ravings in the violent ward of a madhouse, the tragedy would not be more complete than it is.

[1] Hauptmann, with many modern dramatists, uses great freedom in the descriptive subtitles of his plays. *Die Weber* he calls a *Schauspiel, Vor Sonnenaufgang* a *soziales Drama, Einsame Menschen* simply a *Drama*, etc.

For the exhibition of Rose's soul-life for which alone the author had care, the above-mentioned exciting finales are unnecessary. And perhaps Hauptmann has never before rounded out the portrait of a human soul in such surely drawn lines; certainly not since *Fuhrmann Henschel.* Like *Die Weber, Hannele, Michael Kramer,* in fact, like all Hauptmann's plays, *Rose Bernd* is an outflow of his deep human commiseration.

The story is as sad as it is short and common. Flamm, mayor of the village, falls in love with his invalid wife's helper, a buxom, fine-looking, joyous-hearted peasant girl. Accidentally the relations between master and servant are discovered by Streckmann, a vain, unscrupulous woman-hunter, who puts the usual price on his silence. The girl refusing to comply is hounded by him and made to suffer unspeakably. Finally she is entrapped and outraged. Even then the persecution does not cease. Rose's father sues the scoundrel for slandering his daughter's character. Rose called upon to testify against Streckmann is ashamed to tell the truth and makes a false oath. Flamm, believing in Rose's bad conduct with other men, generously acquits himself of the blame for her ruin; his wife, who has nobly stood by Rose, now also weakens in her sympathy. At last Rose Bernd breaks down under the terrible strain of so many sorrows. In a lonely field she gives birth to a child which in her frenzied anguish she strangles. Then she is arrested. At this point the play leaves off; wisely, for the verdict of legal justice would necessarily carry a dissonance into our mood, attuned as nearly to pure compassion as that of Rose's deeply devout betrothed from whom the revelation of her deed wrings the pitying final words of the play: *Das Mädel — was muß die gelitten han!* (" The lass — how she must have suffered!")

However much one is impressed by this last effort of Hauptmann, yet it is not the work of transcendent dramatic merit which his countless admirers have been expecting from him year after year, to be disappointed again and again. The excellences of Hauptmann's later plays do not wholly compensate for certain inherent defects which make it look as though he were debarred by his make-up from the achievement of unqualifiedly great works. He is not destined, apparently, to be the Messiah of the German stage.

Hauptmann's literary characteristics have been fully treated in the beginning of this chapter; it is therefore not necessary to revert to a discussion either of his powers or of his failings. All in all, though disinclined to join in the song of boundless praise that is raised to Gerhart Hauptmann by a many-voiced and ever-swelling chorus, we gladly honor him in spite of his limitations as one of the greatest poets of his time and country. Lest our position towards his work should have seemed at all lacking in the reverence justly due to a writer of his rank and sincerity, we want to repeat the belief, set forth in an early portion of this chapter, that Hauptmann in cultivating the drama to the exclusion of every other literary form lets the richest acres of his genius lie fallow, and we plead, in extenuation of the critical attitude taken, a certain resentful sense of disappointment. Nietzsche once said of Wagner: " I believe it often happens that artists do not realize what they are best able to do because they are too vain." One cannot help pointing the aphorism at Hauptmann. He is at his happiest when letting his emotional nature break out into poetic strains. He could be the prince among modern lyrists if he would. That is why we clamor for songs from him — he gives us nothing but dramas.

On the other hand, if from the world of hopes and ideals we turn our eyes to that of results and realities, we may well be proud of Gerhart Hauptmann. At the age of forty-two he has to his credit an imposing array of performances. His artistic creativeness is not past its heyday. A richer development may yet lie before him: a growth in character, intellect, and artistic ability. We have much reason to be grateful to him for what he has already given; and since ideal hopes will not be suppressed, who shall keep us from looking for still greater gifts?

[Hauptmann's latest play, *Elga*, appeared after the plates of this volume were ready for the press, so that it could not be included in the review.]

MODERN
GERMAN LITERATURE

WOMEN WRITERS

WOMEN WRITERS OF THE NINE-TEENTH CENTURY

It is the prevailing practice of historians of German literature to maintain a somewhat rigid separation of sexes, in their classification of writers. There is thus some precedent for the not altogether philosophic procedure of the present paper, in segregating a number of writers by virtue of their sex for a separate critical treatment. In respect to quantity, the contribution made by women in the field of German letters in the nineteenth century is sufficiently enormous to justify such a segregation. And there is a certain continuity of development running through the whole of it which makes it well worth while to consider the *Frauenschriftstellerei* of the century by itself.

The general critical judgment passed upon the great bulk of it will not fall wide of this verdict: A startling absence of freshness and originality, counterbalanced in a measure by a great imitative faculty. Naturally we wonder where the cause of the limitation may lie. In Germany it may be that absorption in domestic interests has been a chief cause for that fatal want of outlook and that seeming incapacity for the fullest self-expression which exclude the greater part of feminine fiction from the legitimate domain of letters. But are the arrested development of the artistic impulse and the atrophy of the higher intellectual powers really to be held alone responsible for the defective literary performance of the German woman? A glance at the writers of other countries gives rise to doubt. In England, George Eliot has remained the only great novelist. George Sand has been without a successor in France. And in the United States, where a well-organized woman-worship has fostered a greater independence, and where opportunities for education have certainly been ample, not a single work of art of the grander stamp has to this day emanated from woman. Whether, then, there be any nature-ordained limitations which deny to woman the gift of truly creative achievement is a matter regarding which, at the outset of this review, we may ask permission to keep our judgment in suspense.

The history of the literary activity of the German woman prior to the nineteenth century, when she made her official bow in polite literature, can be gathered only by indirection, namely, by ascertaining the extent of her influence over literary art. Beyond a doubt there always has existed, under some guise or other, a measure of feminine control over letters. For instance, in both classic periods women were a dominant force: *Minne-dienst* (the "service of the lady") is the mainspring of nearly all German lyrics to the end of the thirteenth century; and even the great epic writers of the Hohenstaufen era are exponents of the chivalric code of love; notably does *Tristan und Isolde* breathe its spirit.

Sterner and less romantic times put an end to this feminine influence of the golden age. It reappeared in a more rational form in the course of the eighteenth century. Womankind has an unassailable title to our gratitude because of the fact that the discreet censorship which imposed upon the maturer works of our classic writers their wonderful artistic reserve lay in the hands of women. The feminine influence it is that lay also at the root of ideal conceptions like Iphigenie, Leonore, Dorothea, Johanna. The women of Weimar and Jena, and elsewhere too, represented an extraordinarily fine culture of mind and taste. The copious volumes of correspondence of the closing eighteenth and the opening nineteenth century, which are among the most genuine human documents of times intellectually so much alive, disprove finally the self-satisfied allegation that the credit for the advanced literary culture of women belongs to the declining nineteenth century, and is mainly due to America.

But literary culture is not necessarily latent genius.

The imitative character of feminine authorship to which reference was made above is attested by the rush of feminine contributions to every variety of fiction, once its era has been fully ushered in. The misery of the woman of letters dearly loves company.

The performances of the female satellites of the classic writers need not be taken up in this place. A catalogue of empty names and titles would be the only yield. None of them has left an ineffaceable impression. Even the one hundred and twenty-five volumes of fiction by Henriette Hanke — who remembers the name? — are incased in solid, impenetrable oblivion. Perchance a passable poem here and there by Luise Brachmann, who leans hard upon the manly shoulders of Schiller, survives. Suffice it to say, in order to gain a starting point, that about the beginning of the nineteenth century feminine fiction came into vogue. Almost immediately it divided into two sorts, between which we have to distinguish to this day. Crudely we may designate these classes as mere amusement novels and novels with a purpose, — a purpose which may be purely artistic, but is, as a rule, educational. It cannot, of course, be said that books of the former class disclaim all ethical tendency whatever. On the contrary, the authors champion the accepted maxims of respectable society and prepare them *in usum Delphini* or rather Delphinæ, since they purvey them to the *Backfisch* or *höhere Tochter*, the "young person" of Germany. It is fiction of this sort that has attached a rather odious sense to the word *Frauenchriftstellerei*. Not, indeed, on any moral grounds. For the somewhat sugary morality of the authoress of this class is unimpeachable, and the most exacting Sunday-school superintendent will cheerfully testify to the soundness of her religious convictions. Nor is a theory of life lacking, either. It conforms to that benedictory optimism of which Mr. Howells claims to have discovered the ordinary cause in an uncommonly well-cooked dinner. Not a drop of bitterness ever makes its way from such a gentle heart to the pen. Bad people, to be sure, there be, presumably for the sake of variety in the color scheme of the universe, and things do have a way of sometimes going wrong. But the lady writer's unalterable forgivingness wears out the most unremitting persecutions of a hounding fate; and to have retribution meted out to him by this sweet soul, the villain must indulge in veritable antics of wickedness. She much more enjoys praying for him, and he, like Editha's improbable burglar, likes to have himself occasionally converted, for a spell. Yet one can ill afford simply to brush aside these "like-mother-used-to-make" novels, because a very large portion of our contemporary fiction, here as well as in Germany, is concocted after the same recipe, from the same mush and milk, and with the same well-greased kitchen utensils. Moreover, it is unfortunately to this class of books that Americans owe their supposed knowledge of the German woman. Externally she consists mainly of a pair of soulful blue eyes, a brace of uncommonly heavy flaxen tresses, a sweet smile, and a Gretchen bag. Her intellectual horizon is marked out

by her accomplishments. She reads and recites
Schiller and the expurgated Heine — over her
fine embroidery; she sings and plays — Schu-
bert, Mendelssohn, and a family sort of Schu-
mann; it remains to say that she knows French
and English and is inordinately fond of the ap-
proved varieties of flowers. She is the famed
angelic maid, the clinging damsel without a back-
bone whom, according to Helene Böhlau, the German loves so dearly. According to that writer
she meets the world with naïvely astonished eyes,
and on the whole manages to have an easy time
of it, for a thousand knights-errant are dying to
discover her and to make her — make them happy.

Yet in fairness to the Germans it must be said
that women of a taller mental stature and a larger
temperamental gamut have long ere yesterday
stepped in front of this anæmic doll and cast
eclipse upon her; and that as a novel-heroine
she is now suffered to smirk and simper on the
bookshelves of the penny circulating libraries
in her own fatherland, or to be translated into
English by Mrs. Caspar Wister.

Let us first turn our attention to the *Tendenz-
schriftstellerei* of women writers. Though exceedingly few women have excelled in literature

by easy mastery of the higher craftsmanship, by
that power of intense concentration and seizure of human nature in which the great writer
reveals himself, yet many have shown an uncommon intellectual force of the aggressive kind.
On the whole, it may be averred without undue
exaggeration that nearly all women who play
a conspicuous rôle in German letters write in a
reformatory frame of mind. And that in a great
majority of cases the woman's cause is their chosen field of effort goes almost without saying.
It is natural, also, that these spirited innovators
come to the front mostly in periods of unrest,
when fiction becomes the theater of a heated
social warfare. At such times the vigilant woman
of the pen contrives under cover of literary exertions to wrest from the turmoil a fresh morsel
of liberty for her sex. This helps explain why
even the female adherents of romanticism did not
subscribe to the political and religious Toryism
into which the movement issued. The emotional
Bettina von Arnim exhibits much of the specifi-
cally romantic extravagance of sentiment; and in
the greatest virtue of romanticism, the capacity
for poetic experience, she also excels. Her more
than half fictitious " Correspondence of Goethe

with a Child " is certainly one of the finest products of German romanticism. Yet in many of
her political and religious views she is in full
accord with " Young Germany." *Dies Buch ge-
hört dem König* (" This Book is for the King ")
is a bold manifesto calling attention in a marked
manner to the starving condition of the Silesian
weavers [1] and blaming a great deal of needless
human misery upon bureaucratic quackery.

The active period of Young Germany extended from the Paris July Revolution (1830)
to the outbreak of the German Revolution of
1848. The momentous social forces that were
enlisted in the onslaught of this school of writers
against the castle of conservatism lent a practical
significance to the cry for the " emancipation "
of woman. The Young Germans, accepting the
doctrines of the French socialists, and familiar
with the writings of St. Simon and George Sand,
which had shed a new light upon the civic relation of the sexes, first set up the audacious demand for civil marriage. It reverberates in all
keys and modulations through the works of the
women of Young Germany, from its sane and
clear phrasings by Fanny Lewald to the more

[1] See p. 149 of this volume.

than indiscreet Utopianisms of the Free Love advocates. For soon not only the sacrament but also the civil institution of marriage was put in doubt; so that even radicals were frightened back by the meaning with which "emancipation," now the watchword for the final purpose of the feminine rebellion, was invested by extremists. We see, then, that towards the middle of the century which has been called a century of democracy, the rising sense of personality permitted the wildest anarchism to run riot within a regenerative scheme which was essentially collectivist; a phenomenon which makes us question whether socialism and individualism are not after all but emanations of one and the same fundamental impulse.

The uncontrolled vagaries of the fanatical emancipationist did much to alienate general sympathy from the rational aims of more clear-eyed leaders. The "advanced woman" of to-day, were she to study these feminine contributions of the Young German and the subsequent literatures, could not fail to be amazed at the modernness of the cures for the ailments of society that are advertised. Julie Burow, for example, urges every woman to adopt a trade or a profession for the sake of material independence. And Luise Otto, the founder of the *Allgemeiner Deutscher Frauenverein* ("General Union of German Women") (1855), even advocates the organization of workingwomen of every grade through labor unions.

We may roughly classify the propagandist fiction of the revolutionary and post-revolutionary period according to the great undercurrents that run through its social philosophy, the collectivist and the individualist; in a third class might be gathered the writings of the opposition, reactionary either from conviction or from inertia and indifference. But such a simple classification must confess itself far too crude to do more than draw attention to the most obvious distinctions.

The contrast between the main forces within the Young German school is tellingly exemplified in Ida Hahn-Hahn and Fanny Lewald. Their lives reach from the beginning of the century to the beginning of the new era in Germany. Fanny Lewald lived from 1811 to 1889. Countess Ida Hahn-Hahn was born in 1805 and died in 1880, — much too late for the good of her literary fame. She had a most tensely eccentric or *Byronesque* temperament, as they used to say

in the days of her prime. The experiences of
her childhood, her matrimonial misfortunes, her
conversion to Catholicism, her brief novitiate
in a convent, and other romantic interludes
show her personal career to have been so intimately connected with the fate of her heroines
that Hahn-Hahn's novels may be considered
as links in a long autobiographic chain. From
the beginning — *Aus der Gesellschaft* (" From
the Realm of Society ") (1838) — she elected
German high life as a congenial field, and by
vouchsafing her readers the coveted peep into
that glittering Vanity Fair she easily attained
popularity. In reading Hahn-Hahn you are
made to feel distinctly that you belong to the
misera plebs. You have bought a ticket that
admits to the gallery only, and are now looking
down upon the dazzling assembly with all of a
plebeian's delight. And as if to show you that
your confidence was not misplaced, the noble
Countess herself stands at the door below scru-
tinizing the arrivals and counting their quarter-
ings. No hero passes muster before her unless
he is at least a baron and can present himself in
a cavalry uniform or in court attire. Commoner
and civilian are admitted only upon absolute

proof of genius, which for the Countess seems
to consist of an indefinite expansiveness. A
genius, in Hahn-Hahn's estimation, is one whose
soul is capable of "immensity." To everything
that is plain, from clothes to character, the lady
has an unconquerable aversion. Her faultlessly
well-groomed men and her stupendously milli-
nered women oscillate between ballroom and bou-
doir as the natural poles of mundane existence.
Oddly enough, in this painted and perfumed world
of the formalities, the most startlingly unconven-
tional things continually do happen. The Countess
revels in tragedies of the soul — as she understands them. To us of to-day Hahn-Hahn's people, fidgeting forever in their heart struggles,
seem somewhat like fishes floundering on the
hook, and we regard them without any real human
pity. But her books have, in spite of their glaring
paradoxes, which are aggravated by a want of the
higher technical requisites, a certain fascination
in that the morbid subjectivity of the hysterical
authoress is astoundingly revealed amidst all the
gorgeous trappings. By virtue of this frankness,
and it alone, she is decidedly modern. Countess
Ida Hahn-Hahn draws from life and goes to the
mirror in quest of models. Heinrich Heine is

authority for the statement that the German authoress writes with only one eye on her page, since the other is fixed on some man. It will be seen that his criticism does not apply to the Countess Hahn-Hahn. Her heroines are all of them Countesses Ida Hahn-Hahn: gushing enthusiasts, doting but capricious lovers, fanatical devotees. They are drowned in a sea of emotional conflicts, and the Countess erects for each of them a tombstone with the epitaph: Genius did it. The modern reader, to be sure, will exculpate genius and lay the blame on an impish impulsiveness of temperament. An instance is the fate of "Faustine," the truest reflex of the authoress herself. Faustine tears her bleeding heart from the grasp of her first lover to pass it from hand to hand and finally, for a rest cure, to take it to a nunnery. Her pernicious life philosophy is contained in this rich epigram: "To love is to devote oneself to a single object; but why should that object always be the same?"

Hahn-Hahn, by the strongly individualistic tendency, foreshadows the *Herrenmoral* rampant in the literature of to-day. That is to say, she is a prophetess of "emancipation" for which the Young Germans, notably Gutzkow and Laube, were striving; but the enlarged freedom is not offered to the men or women of ordinary caliber, the *Vielzuvielen* of Nietzsche. No; it is exclusively a prerogative of the exceptional person; or, in Stirner-Nietzschean phraseology, of *der Einzige* or *der Eigene.* Only — this is Hahn-Hahn's personal note — the exceptional man, the great personality, happens regularly to be an aristocrat.

Over against this unreasoned accentuation of aristocratic egotism may be placed the democratic altruism of Fanny Lewald. The sober qualities which make this bourgeoise of Jewish extraction a potent educational factor in the *Frauenbewegung* (woman movement), render her distinctly unromantic and, it must be confessed, a trifle prosy. The motive power of her convincing eloquence is not a fiery temperament, but cool logic. She is clear and definite, always temperate, and severely judicial, hence the reforms which she advocates are within the bounds of reason. She ponders the same problems as Ida Hahn-Hahn, but with greater impartiality and depth. The tendency of her contemporaries to exempt the genius from the common moral obligations had a formidable opponent in Fanny Lewald.

She studied the much-discussed marriage question in such a fair and sober spirit that her novel *Eine Lebensfrage* (" A Question of Life ") (1845), one of the earliest and most direct literary arguments in favor of divorce, commanded general attention and respect. Among the earlier champions of the "new woman," Fanny Lewald deserves the first place of honor. Her successful practical activities for the advancement of the cause of women were in full accord with her literary work.

It is only natural that the aims of the radical women should have stricken horror to pious Protestant souls like Marie Nathusius, the conservative and orthodox authoress of the *Tagebuch eines armen Fräuleins* (" Diary of a Poor Gentlewoman") (1853). This exquisitely "inward" book breathes wholly the humble spirit of obedience which would not meddle with the affairs of the world, believing them safe enough in the hand of Providence.

On the Catholic side the projects of Young Germany are viewed with even greater alarm, as, for instance, by Annette von Droste-Hülshoff (1797–1848), the most remarkable woman writer of her generation, and in the judgment of many

competent critics the foremost among all German
poets of her sex. Droste's real strength, however,
does not lie in the defense of her traditional ideals,
of which, by the way, she regards George Sand as
the arch enemy. On the contrary, the "purpose"
in her books, springing from bigotry and a certain
religious mysticism, overcasts her artistic clear-
ness and is the very feature that forbids unqualified admiration. For the self-repression in Droste's
works is much more than artistic restraint. The
mistiness of the composition makes us conscious
of her want of outlook. This limitation is compensated in Droste's novels by an uncompromising veracity and rare minuteness of observation,
powers which qualified this daughter of the "red
soil" of Westphalia to become our first great
representative of "regional" art. Still greater
is Droste in her lyrics. They are a fascinating blend of rugged strength of character and
delicacy of perception, and reveal an amazing
nature-sense which knows how to express the
personality of the meanest object of nature. In
reproducing her sensuous impressions of an en-
semble such as a landscape, the poetess calls
up in the reader novel experiences of nature, in
which respect she may rightly be called an early

impressionist, a forerunner of such moderns as Gabriele d'Annunzio.

Likewise averse to the participation of women in public life is another powerful lyrist, the Viennese Betty Paoli (1815–1894). Her poetry betrays much more frankly than Droste's its motive power:

> Ich bin nichts weiter als ein Herz,
> Das viel gelebt und viel gelitten.

She might have said *geliebt* instead of *gelebt*, and come nearer to the truth. In poems full of intense yet rather reflective passion she discountenances all feminine ambition; woman can find her only chance of happiness in love, self-effacing love. Nature has thus circumscribed her lot, but has at the same time endowed her with a power of blissful self-surrender far beyond any of which the coarser-grained organization of man is capable.

From these serious writers we must now turn aside for a moment to the two most prolific women writers of the entire nineteenth century, writers who manifest an attitude of unruffled placidity towards questions of ethical import, of which stoicism the last secret is stolid indifference.

Luise Mühlbach (1814–1873) stood quite apart from the triumphs and defeats of Young Germany, although she was married to a prominent member of that school. Seldom before the days of our now fortunately expiring craze for "historical" romance has the vogue of a writer so far outstripped his merits as was the case with Mühlbach. She was certainly not without considerable talent; but she was utterly devoid of artistic stability, and permitted her ruinously facile pen to run away with her literary conscience. Yet this ungoverned quill-driver had her most loyal readers amongst the cultured classes, because her novels were perfectly suited to the shallow taste for historical anecdote that prevailed for a long time after the revolution of 1848. As a matter of fact, her characters had as faint a resemblance to their originals as the mute procession men in a Shakespearean play bear to the figures they represent: they only paraded in their masks and clothes. Mühlbach's first phenomenal success in the field of historical romance was "Frederick the Great and his Court" (1854), a novel in thirteen interminable parts. After that, under the spur of increasing popularity, she averaged a baker's dozen of volumes a year. The whole field of modern history was canvassed for its backstair gossip. There is hardly a famous personage of the eighteenth or nineteenth century up to Frederick III whom Mühlbach did not cut up and serve up in her literary kitchen. Under her real name (Frau Professor Mundt) she enjoyed in Berlin a reputation as a capital cook and saving housekeeper. But although her domestic economy extended also to her literary work and she spread her heroes thin enough so as to make them go the farther, yet before the hand of death stopped her pen, at the age of sixty, the limited supply had practically given out, and during her last years she was forced to rehash the old favorites.

Misfortune never comes single. Charlotte Birch-Pfeiffer (1800–1868) is the Luise Mühlbach of the German drama. For a true dramatist she lacked the first and last requirement, — the power to grasp character; but she knew how to create an effective rôle. She could not invent a plot; but she had great constructive skill of a certain cheap kind, a perfect mastery of the claptrap of the stage, and absolute control over the facial muscles and tear ducts of the groundling. Her plays fairly drip with maudlin sentimentality.

Withal she was very enterprising. Were she
writing in these days, Birch-Pfeiffer might justly
assert her patent to one method of that singular
manifestation of our democracy, the theatrical
trust, for she dramatized every popular novel she
could lay hands on. French and English writers,
such as Dickens, Brontë, Victor Hugo, George
Sand, Bulwer, George Eliot, and home novelists,
as Auerbach, Spindler, and Schücking, were pro-
miscuously prepared for the stage.

In dealing with these famous authoresses one
lapses easily from that dignity which is somehow expected of the literary historian. In extenuation, the Horatian *Difficile est satiram non
scribere* may be pleaded. At any rate, the sum
total of the feminine fiction of the romantic and
the Young German era, as well as of that immediately following, is ill calculated to convert the
skeptic. We behold, on the one hand, an agitation which takes its cues from robust masculine
minds and in the main retails the ideas of others
to the sluggish comprehension of the public.
This is done in most cases without much deference to the dictates of the æsthetic conscience.
Nevertheless one significant change is wrought
out by the feministic drift of this fiction, namely,

the gradual shifting of the center of interest from the hero to the heroine. Having her frequently exorbitant claims refused in the material world, woman transfers them to the realm of fiction. And so, without any great artistic meaning, the novels which women write and women read and in which women are the leading figures furnish an inventory of the feminine aspirations of the period. A great technical gain accrued to this class of books from the increasing power of character observation and growing zest for psychological inquiry. Little by little it came to be realized that the best judge of the moral organization of woman is woman herself, and when this recognition was eventually coupled with the analytic skill of to-day, then at last the conditions were ripe under which alone the German authoress was able to seize woman's life in its fullness.

Quite in contrast to the purpose novel stands the huge mass of mere amusement fiction, which has been characterized above.[1] Throughout the century its output is mainly regulated by the commercial law of demand and supply. By the middle of the century this kind of novel-writing, being then practically the one outlet for the "intellectual"

[1] See pp. 235–237.

ambition of women, had taken on the aspect of
a teachable and learnable trade. Public taste had
settled into a comfortable sameness, and from now
on the technical accomplishments of the artisan
novelists were quite equal to the claims made on
their talents. The woods of fiction land were peo-
pled by permanent and accommodating settlers.
The intending authoress need only shake a tree
and down came the baron or officer or professor
or artist that was wanted, and the subsidiary characters were equally obliging in dropping down
ready made and just as good as new. Even the
plot and the diction were cut and dried. With
the aid of the family magazines, among which *Die
Gartenlaube* and *Über Land und Meer* marked the
highest level tolerated by the " general reader," the
conventionalized novel as well as the conventionalized lyric predominated throughout the third
quarter of the nineteenth century in distressing
uniformity. But we only have to think of such
books as Winston Churchill's *The Crisis* in order
to see what an astonishing success smiles frequently upon works of this order. As for the
" tendency," it must not be supposed that the pas-
time fiction has n't any. We find it wholly con-
cordant with the general way of thinking. The

great majority of these writings display a species
of mild, dilute liberalism. For after the strenuous
agitation set afloat by Young Germany had suffered shipwreck in the disaster of 1848, its smaller
débris drifted peacefully on the shallow waters of
amusement fiction. In this generation it was con-
ceded that women should strive for freedom, but
the extent or degree of this freedom was a matter
of higgling dispute. So, for instance, the question
was raised, What callings are suitable for a woman?
And it is quite in harmony with the meaning art
then had for a writer like Wilhelmine von Hillern,
the daughter of Charlotte Birch-Pfeiffer, to conclude that the laurels which grow on the tree of
science are beyond the reach of woman, but that
she may pluck her laurels lustily from the tree of
art; as though excellence in art were less difficult
to attain than distinction in science. The "liberalism" of the women novelists shows itself in their
incessant war upon prejudices, but they select
either such prejudices as no longer prevail, or
those which it is safe enough to fight, and, as
a rule, their heart is not in the battle. We have
refrained from discussing specimens of the out-
and-out amusement novel in the earlier half of
the century. For the period that lies between

1848 and the great war of 1870 Luise Mühlbach was given as a type, although she made pretense to position as an "historical" novelist.

The paragon among German authoresses as they were about 1875 is E. Marlitt (her real name is Eugenie John), who illustrates better than she explains the prodigious popularity of a fiction which combined graceful entertainment with easy moralizings, and managed to win applause from the liberals without forfeiting the approval of the conservatives. *Goldelse, Reichsgräfin Gisela, Im Hause des Kommerzienrats, Das Geheimnis der alten Mamsell, Die zweite Frau, Das Heideprinzeßchen,*[1] and the other novels which have helped us to while away many and many a dreary hour under the unsuspecting eye of a drowsy teacher, are not without many prettinesses. Marlitt may justly be called an "accomplished" writer. She possesses the gift of narrative glib and voluble; her morals are delightful; she has a knack for the ready and seemingly natural solution of unsolvable problems; and, best of all, she never forgets her manners.

[1] The English titles given these books by Mrs. C. Wister are: "Gold Elsie," "Countess Gisela," "At the Councilor's," "The Old Mam'selle's Secret," "The Second Wife," "The Little Moorland Princess."

But even the naïvely admiring eyes of the vora-
cious novel-reader cannot long remain shut
against certain defects of Marlitt, though these
may seem to him mere specks of imperfection.
There is in her stories an engine-turned uniformity of plot and an unnecessarily harsh prejudice
against common sense. The reason is not far to
seek. Common sense, were it not resolutely suppressed as a factor in her plots, might make itself
disagreeable by standing in the way of the all-is-
well conclusion required by an exacting public.
It is, accordingly, treated as a negligible quantity, and the director-generalship of human affairs
in Marlitt's novels devolves upon the generous
promptings of the human heart. Chief aid-de-
camp to the noble heart is the irresistible
attractiveness of all good people. Whereas in
life victories are usually won through powerful
exertion or strong-willed self-denial, in Marlitt
the spring of personal magnetism is touched, the
good heart does the rest, and stern truth may
whistle for it. This successful method could not
long remain Marlitt's secret. Once discovered,
it was caught up by a swarm of busy imitators
who learned the trick though they missed the
grace, and to this day their widely ramified

sorority flourishes in all parts of the globe. But
lest we be diverted too long from our subject,
which is, after all, a literary one, let us dismiss
the host of Marlitt's satellites with brevity. It
is but fair, however, not to make this jejune and
time-serving class too inclusive. E. Werner, for
instance, deserves to be excepted. She adopted
in a general way Marlitt's method of dyeing in
fine colors. But as a writer she eventually surpassed her model, thanks to a greater breadth
of horizon, warmth of conviction, and a certain
trenchant critical faculty. Instead of limiting
herself to the conventional assortment of heroes,
she showed a kindly attachment for misfit individuals; this even betrayed her occasionally into
representing an unmitigated crank as a hero.
One might easily mention a number of other
popular women novelists of the past generation
who, like Werner, can lay claim to a high degree
of skill and, without being in any sense great
writers, wield a good and steady pen at the business. To name only a few, a commendable brisk-
ness of style marks the stories of Golo Raimund,
Egon Fels, Emmy von Dincklage, and Claire
von Glümer. Still more independently gifted are
Sophie Junghans and Emilie Junker.

To none of these authors of the seventies, however, but perhaps to Luise von François, belongs the distinction of having contributed to the permanent fund of literature the first book of lasting worth. *Die letzte Reckenburgerin* ("The Last Lady of Reckenburg") presents with surprising realism a picture of patriarchal existence at the end of the eighteenth and the beginning of the nineteenth century. Despite its main shortcomings, which consist in a tendency to preach in season and out of season and the want of outlook so common in feminine fiction, *Die letzte Reckenburgerin* must be assigned a high place among German novels, not only by comparison with the average, but on account of its own unmistakable merit. It is the product of a penetrating, energetic, yet gentle and forgiving mind.

From now on women writers of real worth become much less rare.

An intellect of the same noble type as François' is revealed in the literary personality of Malwida von Meysenbug, whose three volumes of memoirs are replete with deepest human interest, since they are the record of a human soul that has ever aligned itself on the spiritual side

of life and has been very close to such eminent
men of the age as Richard Wagner and Friedrich Nietzsche. Meysenbug and François belong
to a group of authoresses who are deeply intellectual and who yet show themselves independent of the "cause," because to them the sole
object worth striving for and the one on which
they have steadily fixed their gaze, is the fuller
development of the idealistic side of human
nature.

A like educational aim, ever consistently idealistic, inspires the work of Marie von Ebner-
Eschenbach, who, now in her seventy-fifth year,
belongs on the whole to the older literary school,
but has in some ways exercised great influence over
the present generation of authoresses. She enjoyed
a rather modest renown before the arrival of the
new era, but once the amiable superficiality of
Marlitt had begun to pall, Ebner-Eschenbach's
depth of feeling was hailed as a welcome relief.
She is now looked upon by some critics as the
foremost novelist of Germany, and by general
consent is recognized as one of the best short-
story writers in the world.

Marlitt and her followers derived much public
approbation from their "idealism." Marie von

Ebner-Eschenbach is an idealist of a much more substantial sort. She is deeply in earnest and permits herself no dalliance in philosophical problems that are beyond her depth. A rare gift of self-criticism is coupled in her with a freedom from prejudice that is almost startling in a member of the high aristocracy.[1] Inborn goodness and the large-mindedness bred of wisdom are the chief elements in the thinking and forgiving morality of her works. In her stories each individual is permitted to struggle in his own unhackneyed way with the problems that beset the path of life, but the course of fate is not deflected by any silly shrinking from an unhappy ending. The guiding hand of the authoress shows only in that the outcome invariably vindicates the higher ethics. That is because she herself stands unswervingly for the Hellenic and Goethean ideal of *Sophrosyne*. This philosophic temperance explains the full meaning of her trivial-sounding motto: *Gutsein ist Glück*. Such high personal qualities are only too apt to put the critic off his guard when it comes to judging the artist in the superior woman. It is at this point that many a thinking reader will feel

[1] By birth she is an Austrian countess.

constrained to part company with the chorus of eulogists. He will not deny at all that Ebner's writings mirror, as has been aptly said, " the conscience of a priestess and the heart of a mother." But he will often miss the distinctive art note. Ebner's composition is apt to be crude or labored; her diction is refractory; in nearly every story a didactic elevation of the voice disturbs the harmony; and as for her realism, it is wholesome and unstudied, but touched up too highly with romantic tints to be convincing. Yet she may claim for her eclecticism as much of truth as is obtained by the "naturalists," for her endeavor, so she tells us, is to reproduce convincingly what she alone has seen: "a noble feature in the face of the outcast, or a flash of genius in the dullard's eye." Marie von Ebner-Eschenbach, to be a writer of the first order, lacks two essentials: a deeper sense of beauty and greater possibilities of temperament. But taken all in all, she is an eminent literary character with a forcible and steadfast individuality of her own.

François, Ebner-Eschenbach, and Meysenbug, although their writings derive their value in part from their pedagogical message, do not pay any particular attention to the woman movement, which, as we saw, stirred so many minds to their depths towards the middle of the century and, after ebbing away in the sands of the later amusement fiction, was to leap forth with fierce vigor in the feminine writings of our own day. The lives and works of these authoresses reflect the waning light of a day aglow with the rich and mellow culture of the Goethean age. In connection with them should be mentioned Carmen Sylva, the Queen of Rumania. She combines the mature temperance of Eschenbach and Meysenbug with the greater intensity of the modern school. To a greater extent even than Marie von Ebner she is a reflective writer. Following W. Jordan's example, she boldly makes the modern scientific theory of the world the intellectual content of her work. As the result of earnest study of social and religious problems her stanch but by no means uncritical optimism stands on the lofty level of an ardent faith in natural evolution.

Having, after this hurried retrospect, now reached the threshold of the present era, we next pass on to a group of younger writers, real transition types that usher in a rather hysterical cultus of art and the artist.

Ada Christen, Ossip Schubin, and Maria Janitschek are all three Austrians, but though not
untinged with the easy-going, sanguine temperament of the modern Phæaces, their conception
of life, on the whole, is dismal enough to suit
the most stringent pessimist. This fundamental
dolefulness sounds most genuine in Ada Christen, the oldest of the trio. Of the same age with
Carmen Sylva, she is grouped with younger
writers because she has even more in common
with them than the Queen of Rumania. Her
impassioned verses in many respects remind one
strongly of Betty Paoli, save that Christen's self-
revelation is much more thoroughgoing: her
poems conceal and disguise nothing. It is a
far cry from the unreserved candor of her *Lie-
der einer Verlorenen* to the pathological " exhi-
bitionism " of Marie Madeleine's *Auf Kypros*
and the lyric confessions of Else Galen-Gube.
And yet, for good or for evil, Ada Christen first
broke the seven sacred seals and bared undi-
vulged feminine secrets. This unrestricted subjectivity is, however, not the only quality which
puts her in a class with the "moderns"; she
belongs there likewise by her harrowing naturalism in depicting the proletarian *milieu*. This is

true both of her verses and her stories. Nevertheless, the famous Viennese humor does not fail her, and some of her homely good-natured stories of Viennese life are veritable cabinet pieces; for example, *Echte Wiener* (" True Children of Vienna "), the story of Waltz King Strauss' boyish infatuation for the mother of the authoress. Ada Christen fully appreciates the quick and lively freshness of Viennese life, yet she grasps the fact that at the root of its artistic *laissez faire* there lies the shallow self-indulgence of the philistine. And in some of her gloom-steeped stories she shows how the native joyousness of such people is overspread by darkening sorrow and finally put out by despair.

The earliest specimens of the work of Ossip Schubin (Lola Kirschner) were full with the promise of great things. They gave evidence of a strong though undisciplined native talent, uncommon dash, a quick power of observation, and showed a keen knowledge of two opposite worlds, high life and the peasantry, truly astonishing in a youthful person and an outsider to both. Ossip Schubin made her literary début at sixteen, and set out on her career with the cheering approval of George Sand and Ivan

Turgenieff. But as time went on and popularity gave her assurance, she seemed to neglect her further artistic education. At any rate she has yet to make good her extraordinary promise. Her present style of writing is calculated to strengthen rather than disarm the suspicion that Ossip Schubin bears some unfortunate affinity to Hahn-Hahn. Not alone in her controlling weakness for international high life; for she is, besides, self-conscious and given to mannerisms — take the polyglot titles of her books — and sensational effects. With the naturalist tendencies she is, on the whole, out of touch, although at the outset of her career she showed a strong leaning towards realism; and although herself quite outspoken in dealing with those subjects which were formerly tabooed in feminine fiction, she has no patience with the extent to which the ruling freedom of speech is made use of by the latest generation of women writers.

This brings me to a feature of the new feminine fiction which even here cannot go wholly unmentioned. The quality for which above all others the German reader was once accustomed to look in the works of women, namely, that maidenly modesty which for sweet souls like

Ottilie Wildermuth and the enterprising Elise Polko still proves such a sure pathfinder to the Christmas tree of the boarding-school miss, is no longer characteristic of the authoress. Extremes often meet. Our women novelists were at one time squeamish. They are now frank beyond the frankness of Amélie Rives-Chanler and Ella Wheeler Wilcox, frank to the very limits of brutality, nay, even to the extent of sometimes overstepping them.

The serious student of literature must not be prudish. But though callous to those transgressions which bring down upon many excellent books the condemnation of our public librarians, even he will be nonplused by the unbridled candor of Maria Janitschek. He will shrink from it only the more because it struts along in pontifical robes. Maria Janitschek came into prominent notice in the early eighties of the past century as one of the first exponents of "modernism." Her chief characteristic is an emotionalism strangely mixed of "mud and fire." On the one hand, she revels in erotic problems of the most *risqué* sort, dealing with them in a manner of the earth earthy. On the other hand, she is a fanatical votary of symbolism, with a passion for all that is abstruse. Like very many modern German writers, she is also a priestess of the greatest mystification of the nineteenth century, the *Übermensch*-cult established by Friedrich Nietzsche.

The number of Schubin's and Janitschek's satellites is legion. Their names, however, are hardly ever heard out of Germany, except possibly that of Hermione von Preuschen, who may be known in this country, at least as a painter, for her " Mors Imperator " was a conspicuous exhibit in the Woman's Building at the Columbian Fair in Chicago. Her writings are as coquettishly mystical as her pictures.

The foregoing synopsis, aiming only at a suggestive and helpful classification, has assumed that a modicum of familiarity with a few of the more conspicuous writers who served as illustrative examples could be taken for granted. Many of their works are accessible in English translations. But now that the critic is at last led into the company of the German woman of letters of to-day, the widespread though unpardonable American ignorance of contemporary German literature confronts him as a serious difficulty; an ignorance which is doubly deplorable on its own account and on account of its causes. This expression of regret does not imply that it is worth while for any one in these busy days to try to keep up with the entire literary production of two continents, with the British Isles thrown in. But a legitimate human interest attaches to whatever part of modern fiction is actually conjured up by the living forces of our time; especially to so much of it as reveals the passing attitude of one generation of men towards the basic principle of society, — the universal moral law. Whatever may otherwise be urged against the new novels and plays of continental Europe, it must be admitted that they have justified their claims on human sympathy by an astoundingly close touch with all sides of life. There is every reason in the world why the literature of to-day should reflect a greater wealth of experience and contain a fuller register of ideas than that of any former period, even though literature has been unable to keep step with the miraculous expansion of the practical activities. Indeed, when viewed from the culture-historic standpoint, the work of living German authoresses is thoroughly worthy of attention. However, there are very few subjects on which even the American woman, superior as she is

to her male compatriot in literary as well as in
general culture, is so densely ignorant. The
reasons are not far to seek. Notwithstanding
her ample educational advantages, the American woman, as a rule, is a poor linguist. To
enjoy a book or a play in the original, one must
at least be beyond the need of continual reference to the dictionary. Yet there are many
otherwise well-educated American women, perhaps just out of college to-day, who are unable
to make out a fairly simple German or French
text. This is to be lamented, even though the
assertion of a living French critic, that to de-
clare oneself unable to read German is to confess
oneself at least twenty years behind the times
in knowledge, is undoubtedly an exaggeration.
Persons unfamiliar with German or French are
very likely to invoke by way of excuse the whim-
sical saying of Emerson, that he would as soon
swim across the Charles River to get to Boston,
instead of crossing the bridge, as he would read
a foreign original when he could obtain a translation. It may be said, in reply to the Concord
sage, that it pays to learn swimming, even apart
from the healthful excitement of the exercise.
For there are some very wide rivers that are

spanned by too few bridges. Such an one is
German literature. Now, it may be asked, how
does it come that so few specimens of German
"modernism" are made accessible to us through
translation? Possibly the explanation lies in the
nonconformity of these audacious Germans to
our tacit exaction that foreign writers should pay
court to our jejunely nice, scrupulously conventionalized literary taste.

The most potent influence that is at work in
the German literature of to-day partakes of the
nature of a grimly resolute striving for the fullest
individual freedom. The effect of the new rebellion sown by the daring genius of Nietzsche is
clearly manifest in the turn taken by the plea,
in fiction, for the woman cause. The rights of
personality, which were formerly subordinated to
considerations of the general welfare, are now
loudly emphasized. The leading women eman-
cipators of to-day extol the "creative" life above
the life sanctioned by social agreement, and do
not question the right of the individual to break
through the accepted moral formulas. They
utterly reject the gospel of patience, which
women love so much to observe and still more
to preach. And while the old accusations of

tyranny are still hurled against the ruling sex
with the undiminished vigor of old, not a little
criticism, intemperate and sometimes savage, is
directed against the meek and stolid submis-
siveness of the women themselves. There is a
degree of danger in this fanatical agitation for
unchecked liberty, and it cannot be denied that
such teaching may prove fatal to a few unsteady
heads. There are two ways of dealing with such
a situation. In this country, where literary fashions bow to the dictate of public opinion, we
choose to suppress the dangerous doctrine by
smothering its utterance in fine indignation. In
Germany, on the other hand, the fullest discussion of heterodoxy is freely tolerated. The Germans realize that progress in culture can only
spring from a soil constantly plowed up by
controversy.

It seems to me, then, that we are committing
a grievous error in denying a hearing to what
the most capable women of Germany have to
say on a subject which to them is of the greatest moment, even though we may feel that their
zeal is greater than their insight. After all, the
heroes and heroines of recent German fiction,
for whom ruthless self-affirmation is claimed as

a special prerogative, are not of the common run of people, but of a class scarcely extant amongst us; they are nearly always artists. And surely we need have little apprehension lest our own types of the overman, the trust magnate and the political boss, catch the infection and apply their overgrown sense of individuality to a sphere other than the material. Candidly, so long as we admit to our homes the "yellow" daily, it is hypocrisy on our part to proscribe any seriously meant book or class of books in the name of public morals.

The literary era that dates from the early eighties of the past century and is commonly called "Youngest Germany" has been more fruitful of good than of evil. Whatever may be our judgment as regards its ethical merits, it has brought us a most gratifying progress in all technical respects. Though the successors of Marlitt in and out of the *Gartenlaube* still jog along imperturbably in the old ruts — St. Keyser, W. Heimburg, D. von Spättgen, F. Kapff-Essenther, H. Schobert, *e tutte quante,*—yet even their banal plots with their never-failing happy dénouement have profited by the modern example. As for the writers of the new school, any fair-minded

person must admire in them a great strength of
purpose and power of observation, a wider range
of sentiment and opinion and a more piercing
artistic vision than were given their predecessors. And while the modern woman of letters
might perhaps resent this congratulation, there
is cause for rejoicing in the fact that the gratifying literary improvement has gone hand in hand
with the steady enlargement of woman's sphere
and opportunities.

In unabated agitation of the woman cause, Gabriele Reuter and Helene Böhlau stand preëmi-
nent. Both strike out boldly for a fuller liberty,
·but they also seek to deepen the sense of woman
towards her new obligations. Reuter's famous
novel, *Aus guter Familie* ("Well Bred"), pleads
in spirited fashion against coercion in every form
whatsoever; by insinuation, the authoress includes
marriage, an institution devised by the despotism
of man and acquiesced in by the slavish cowardice
of woman. The slender thread on which Gabriele
Reuter strings her moralizings is the tragic story
of Agathe Heidling, the daughter of an official.
Like all girls of her class, she is brought up primarily to marry; failing to do this, she settles,
after a brief rebellion, into a purposeless life at

the cost of her true personality, and, finally, of her reason. Incontestably, this book, of which the lesson is self-evident, has proved a powerful lever in the hands of the radical advocates of social reform. Its plea, as is the custom with such books, gained the day not so much by the persuasiveness of the argument as by virtue of its glittering eloquence. Few "novels of purpose," it should be borne in mind, do make their way by means of intrinsic worth; most derive success from vociferation.

Helene Böhlau is no less emphatic than Gabriele Reuter, but very much more forcible. She, too, enjoys writing "at the top of her lungs"; yet even though she has not held aloof from sensational exaggerations, — notably in *Das Recht der Mutter* (" The Mother's Right ") and in *Halbtier* (" Half Beast "), — she is the greater artist of the two. Two entirely different groups of novels have come from her pen. The earlier ones, incited by a close touch with Goethean culture — Helene Böhlau grew up in Weimar — radiate a sunny humor, but bear not at all on vital issues. Later on, Nietzsche supersedes Goethe as Böhlau's lodestar. Henceforth she extols the new, intoxicating passion of life that makes a demigod of him who

will desert beaten paths and, with a new-won
consciousness, gain the power of wresting joy
from each phenomenon as it reveals itself anew.
This sovereign power, to Nietzsche and his disciples, is the sublimated life which alone is worth
living. An almost sacred wrath against the meager
contentment of the female philistine as well as
against the rapacity of her male tyrant burns
in Böhlau's intemperate harangues. Forever she
harps the plaint of *Iphigenie in Tauris: Der
Frauen Zustand ist beklagenswert.* In *Adam
und Eva* or *Halbtier* she maintains that woman
such as she has become through the enforced
disuse of her spiritual faculties is not yet a completed human being. This shows itself, among
other ways, in her pitiable impotence when
brought face to face with adversity. "If a beast
were hunted as woman has been, it would de-
velop a weapon — a horn perchance, or a venom-
ous tooth. Not so woman. She has only grown
tamer and tamer, disgustingly tame, and has become in the veriest sense a beast of burden. Her
direst wants have been neglected. If she has
obtained a small part of her rightful inheritance,
she has done so with the cunning of a famished
beast — by stealth and subterfuge." Every blow

prostrates her, leaving her unsustained by the
consolations of the mind. Woman, according to
Böhlau, is a human body which passes through
life entirely unspiritualized. And that half of
mankind which they call the gentler or weaker
sex is, in truth, the robust, the coarsely material-
istic, inimical perforce to all that is lofty or subtle
in our existence.

Fortunately for woman, so Böhlau holds, her
relentless persecutor, man, is singularly naïve in
his judgment and not at all hard to suit. All
that he expects of her is that she should make
herself as nearly as possible like the ladies he
admires on the front cover of the German family
magazines. But the strong-minded Helene Böhlau scorns and hates the easily pleased despot
and marks him with a fiery cross, by way of a
warning to the sisterhood.

Aside perhaps from her faith in the possibilities of womankind, Helene Böhlau is a thoroughgoing disciple of Nietzsche. As such she sets her
face against the prevailing mope-eyed conception
of human destiny which takes the form of either
complacent optimism or indolent pessimism. To
her way of thinking, the culmination of the fuller
life lies in its supreme moments, be they moments

of achievement or defeat. George Eliot once expresses a similar sentiment when, in *The Mill on the Floss*, she says of the heroine as she nears the climax of her fate: "Even the coming pain could not seem bitter — she was ready to welcome it as a part of life, for life at this moment seemed a keen, vibrating consciousness poised above pleasure or pain." And Ricarda Huch, in a poem, says to Life: *Denn du bist süß in deinen Bitternissen.* It is a maxim with Böhlau that every true personality contains the possibilities of a self-determination that should bring either crowning success or destruction, should lead either to unmingled happiness or — to pure unhappiness.

But —

> Every deed of ours, no less than every sorrow,
> Impedes the onward march of life.
> Some alien substance more and more is cleaving
> To all the mind conceives of grand and fair.[1]

In the humdrum grind of our daily existence, which is bound sooner or later to shatter the exceptional individuality, the human tragedy is adulterated.

---

[1] Goethe, *Faust*, translation by Bayard Taylor.

It will be noted that the writings of Helene
Böhlau, although she is a realist as regards the
striking reproduction of the *milieu*, are steeped
in the azure of idealism. Naturally enough she
takes by preference artists for her heroes and,
like a majority of the novelists of to-day, seeks
her models in the "Athens on the Isar," the center
of the "new art," Munich. This is true both of
Halbtier and of her most important book, *Der
Rangierbahnhof* ("The Switching Station"), certainly one of the greatest novels of recent times.
The plot of this story, again, is made to subserve
the writer's ethical creed. Its central figure, Olly,
burns up with an inner fire which she cannot communicate to the surrounding world. Her family,
including a well-meaning but commonplace and
selfish husband, cannot understand her, and her
inner self is, as it were, placed on an insulating
stool; but at the last, when her wasted young life
is fast slipping away, the companion soul of the
great artist friend stands revealed before her and
she dies contented. The resemblance of this
story to that of Marie Bashkirtseff and Bastien-
Lepage is unmistakable. Yet "The Switching
Station," as may be inferred from the very title,
should in the main be understood symbolically.

Many of our stanchest realists are to be found in the downright symbolist school. Strange as this fact may seem, there is assuredly nothing contrary either to nature or to art in a method whereby the externals are seized for the presentment of the larger truth. But symbolism somehow carries within it the germ of exaggeration. Even Ibsen, the master in combining the two methods, succumbs occasionally to the danger, and falls into an excessive symbolism, as, for instance, in "When We Dead Awake," where the principal characters are little more than allegories mounted on human legs. It is on these same shoals, too, that Böhlau's imposing art is more than once seen to founder.

Then, too, her artistic equipoise is disturbed by her strong desire to retaliate upon the enemy of her sex. Barring a few rather freakish overmen, all specimens of the masculine gender that appear in her late novels are either hopeless reprobates or invertebrate ninnies. The iniquity of man is concededly great and his villainy deep-dyed; when overdrawn by a feminist they border on the grotesque.

It may be pertinent in this place to call attention to a significant change wrought out in these days: the feminine literature of to-day is an integral factor in the general intellectual life; it consequently shares in the literary evolution. Recent German fiction has emerged from the era of uncompromising realism with a zest for psychological inquiry, and in the natural order of things women become more deeply inquisitive about themselves. At the same time they realize more fully than before their special gift and superior aptitude for detailed observation, and to their minute and honest account of themselves we owe an enlarged knowledge of woman's character.[1] But in the reformatory zeal which impels our women writers to redress the wrongs of their sex, the great human problems under discussion do not receive sober study, and so we find that even a writer of Helene Böhlau's stature seems shut out from the loftier outlook from which the true poet views the eternal pantomime.

At the present moment the most conspicuous German authoress is undoubtedly Clara Viebig. She is the leading apostle of the anti-emancipation doctrine of Laura Marholm, — the doctrine that woman is but a fragmentary work of nature, and needs to be completed by the union with

[1] Cf. p. 60.

man. Yet in spite of this theory, Viebig exhibits in her style a rugged, virile strength. In her masterly village stories, *Kinder der Eifel* ("Children of the Eifel"), and in the grimly humorous novel *Das Weiberdorf* (" A Women's Village "), she uncurtains with a pitiless hand the brutalities of peasant life. *Das tägliche Brod* (" Daily Bread ") is a deeply serious study of the servant problem under aspects which to Americans will seem stranger than fiction, they are so different from our own. " The Watch on the Rhine " is a veritable triumph of the *Heimatkunst* (" regional art ") so assiduously cultivated by the Germans. The latest of Viebig's literary performances, the novels *Vom Müllerhannes* (" Jack the Miller ") and *Das schlafende Heer* (" The Sleeping Army ") and a dramatic suite entitled *Der Kampf um den Mann* (" The Fight for a Man ") — all three published within the last two years — are keeping her prominently before the public.

Though overshadowed by Böhlau and Viebig, yet there are many other forceful writers in the younger generation, — women full of indomitable energy, deep convictions, in some cases equipped with a fine technical skill. Only a few of them can here be mentioned.

Anselm (Selma) Heine is, like Helene Böhlau, a realistic symbolist who likes to deal with problems from the artist's sphere. She teaches, among other things, that the higher individuality is put in jeopardy by a too congenial marriage.

With a telling protest against the ruling conventions are fraught the plays and stories of Anna Croissant-Rust and those of the unfortunate Juliana Déry, who sealed her dissension from the accepted social code with a tragic death. Emil Marriot (Emilie Mataja) varies the theme by tracing the real "soul" tragedies to religious conflicts. She is a devout Catholic, yet has a predilection for the very delicate subject of clerical love with which the consummate art of Paul Heyse has dealt in *Zwei Gefangene* (" Two Prisoners "). In the series of short stories, *Mit der Tonsur* (" Tonsured Heads "), the principal characters are priests who are unhappy through love. Perhaps the best thing she has written is the stirring prose threnody *Der Geistliche Tod* (" A Clerical Death ").

Marie Eugenie delle Grazie is a poetess of unquestionable power, but lack of artistic discipline renders her unequal to the great tasks she elects. In her epos " Robespierre " — she is one of the relatively few women who have attempted epic poetry—she demonstrates that even the most terrifying realism is not proof against the noisy sort of emotionalism.

Under her pseudonym of Leo Hildeck, Leonie Meyerhof has made a well-known name for herself. In *Wollen und Werden* (" Purpose and Achievement ") the artist tragedy turns on the discrepancy between the creative impulse and the sustaining capacity for work. Hildeck is an enthusiastic Nietzschean, and the prototype of her *Feuersäule* (" The Pillar of Fire "), notwithstanding her express denial, can be none other than Max Stirner, the forestaller of Nietzsche. For her entirely un-German coldness, this writer compensates by a rare constructive skill.

Lou Andreas-Salomé, the biographer and one-time friend of the great poet-philosopher-madman, deals in a bold, broad manner with intricate psychological subjects, such as the baleful awakening from juvenile illusions, dwelling strongly on the necessity for deep religious sentiment.

The two most promising among the youngest set of German authoresses also follow undoubtedly in Nictzsche's footsteps. The youthful Sophie Hoechstetter is so deeply engrossed in

the propagation of the individualistic creed that
she has taken no time to bestow great care on
the form of her writings; so her rebel pen does
not disdain the handy style and methods of the
amusement novel, even though in the interpretation of the master Zarathustra she exhibits a
greater freedom of thought than most other
disciples.

An even more resolute agitator and by far a
more convincing "realist" is Hans von Kahlenberg, whose real name is Helene von Montbart,
a young woman belonging to the circles that
are styled *Militäradel* ("military nobility"), and
whose novels move accordingly in the higher
strata of German life. It would not be easy to
name a writer of either sex so entirely unsenti-
mental as Hans von Kahlenberg, or one with a
finer ear for the hollowness of "official morality"
and a keener eye for the sores that eat their way
through the German body social. Upon these
cancerous spots she advances composedly with
the surgeon's blade, which she wields in no gin-
gerly way and without first administering anæs-
thetics. Though only in the early thirties, she
is already a master of the naturalistic method.
The crassness in the portrayal of her *milieu*

— e.g. *Die Familie Barchwitz* (" The Barchwitz Family "), *Die Sembritzkys* (" The Sembritzkys"), and other novels — may be easily condoned, in view of her deep sympathy with the sufferings of her people.

The enumeration of the authoresses of this combative Nietzschean sect might be continued to great length. The aim of this sketch, however, cannot be completeness, but at best an indication of salient traits, and enough has been said to substantiate the statement made before with regard to the predominant influence of Nietzsche on our feminine literature of dissent.

Two writers who represent the high-water mark of artistic achievement by German authoresses of the living generation have been reserved to the last. Neither can be classed as a Nietzschean of strict observance, and neither can be called a thoroughgoing realist, or a pedantic symbolist. But to elude classification is to give the sincerest proof of a self-dependent artistic personality. Isolde Kurz and Ricarda Huch come well up to the test. Not uninfluenced, certainly, by great models, but without looking right or left to schools and coteries, they have made their way to the front rank. They are artists, first and last, who have learned to employ the technical acquisitions of the modern school for the presentment of facts under their eternal aspect.

Of the two, Isolde Kurz is perhaps the more versatile. She commands a style which is scarcely surpassed by Paul Heyse when at his best. Her poems, and in a still higher degree her short stories and satirical fairy tales, besides excelling in a chaste plastic beauty of language, win by their rich fund of ripe human wisdom and an irresistible humor, delightful even though spiced with cutting sarcasm, of which the reader himself is frequently made the mark. The extraordinary strength of Kurz's art lies in its burrowing psychology, by which the subtlest qualities and conditions of mind are brought to light. This rare power enables the writer to expose with sensuous truthfulness, "realistically" as it were, the world of the unreal. To quote an example, the story *Mittagsgespenst* ("A Midday Specter") reproduces with great vividness a weird daydream of a mediæval city in the full fierceness of its tempestuous life. Italian life, especially that of the Renaissance, has the same charm for Isolde Kurz that it exercised on her great teacher, Conrad

Ferdinand Meyer. Her most serious contributions to letters, besides a small volume of exquisite lyrics, are two collections of short stories: *Florentiner Novellen* (" Short Stories of Florence ") and *Italienische Erzählungen* (" Italian Tales ").

Of still greater artistic significance is the work of Ricarda Huch. It detracts in no wise from the marvelous originality of her art that it has been influenced by Gottfried Keller and Conrad Ferdinand Meyer, and that it, too, has been electrified by a spark from Nietzsche's wayward genius. The last-mentioned influence is recognized in her favorite heroes. They are the *Lebenskünstler*, the past masters of the art of living, modern Renaissance men and women with a capacity for translating great emotions into action. Huch, at the age of thirty-eight, is the author of fifteen books comprising two metrical plays, two collections of critical essays, a historical study, a book of poems, and nine volumes of fiction. All of these are works of intrinsic value. Her chief title to fame, however, still reposes on *Erinnerungen von Ludolf Ursleu dem Jüngeren* (" Recollections of Ludolf Ursleu the Younger "), a book full of the indefinable charm exhaled only by what the French call *une œuvre de longue haleine;* one of those rare books, that is to say, which draw the reader into the very mood in which they were conceived and sustain him in it. The novelist whose unerring art has given him supreme power of this sort is Thackeray. By virtue of their temperamental consistency, *Pendennis*, *Henry Esmond*, *The Newcomes*, are unsurpassable models. Du Maurier's *Trilby* owes its unquestionable value to close and successful study of those great models. Among living writers, Pierre Loti and Maurice Maeterlinck, by an almost hypnotic power, communicate to the reader their own minor-key temper of mind. Ricarda Huch attains similar effects without the aid of chiaroscuro. At least in *Ursleu* and *Aus der Triumphgasse* ("Stories from Triumph Lane") she draws in the broad light of her own day. As a rule, however, she makes the color perfection of her picture stand forth more distinctly by incasing it in an artistic frame of chaste design. It is no easy matter to adapt, as Huch has done, the style of an old chronicle to a recital of contemporaneous events. But Huch's vigorous art does not choose the line of least resistance. Altogether she compels the highest admiration for her firm conscientiousness in squaring herself with technical difficulties and exacting from herself heroic tasks. It is characteristic, perhaps, that her most ambitious works are by far her best. Whereas the short stories fall appreciably below the high standard by which her superlative art deserves to be marked, her two master novels, by virtue of their flawless structure, excel even Keller's famous *Der grüne Heinrich* ("Green Henry") and take elevated rank with the lofty achievement of Conrad Ferdinand Meyer's imperishable prose epics.

The "Memories of Ursleu" purports to be written in cloistered solitude by the sole representative of a headstrong race whose members, notwithstanding their imperious vital instincts, are doomed to self-destruction by their unbending will. In the unraveling of the plot a most skillful use is made of episode, for the double purpose of enlarging the historical vista and, at the same time, making the private tragedy stand out in bold relief against the general calamity. The action passes in the republic of Hamburg during the cholera epidemic of less than twenty years ago. The plague is not broadly pictured as in Manzoni's *I Promessi Sposi;* rather with the delicate discretion used by Boccaccio in the framing of the *Decamerone.* The "Band of the Holy Life," into which young

patricians of both sexes form themselves in order
to vindicate amid the surrounding horrors of death
the joy of living, serves as a symbol for the chief
tenet in Ricarda Huch's philosophy: life is not
worth living without the illusions; hence let us
cling to the illusions.   No need of saying that
Ricarda Huch is not a "realist" in the pedantic
acceptation of the term.   Yet she knows well how
to reproduce the *milieu* of the patrician life as
well as—in *Aus der Triumphgasse*—of the slums;
and she possesses the highest credential of her
art—style.   *Le style c'est*—this time—*la femme!*
Huch's is a personality with apparently unlimited
possibilities of inward experience and a coextensive power of articulation,—herself a member
of the "Band of the Holy Life," with a passionate desire to taste of the choicest dishes at
the banquet of life.   *Unersättlich* ("Insatiable")
is one of her finest poems which gives adequate
expression to this longing.

> Ganz mit Frühling und Sonnenstrahl,
> Klang und duftendem Blütenguß
> Mein verlangendes Herz einmal
> Füll' mir, seliger Überfluß!
>
> Gib mir ewiger Jugend Glanz,
> Gib mir ewigen Lebens Kraft,

Gib im flüchtigen Stundentanz
Ewig wirkende Leidenschaft!

Aus dem Meere des Wissens laß
Satt mich trinken in tiefem Zug!
Gib von Liebe und gib von Haß
Meiner Seele einmal genug.

With this cursory characterization of the most important German women writers of the hour this sketch may be concluded. It goes without saying that many deserving books have necessarily been left undiscussed, and that of many well-known authoresses even the names could not be mentioned. To furnish a handy reference catalogue was not the reviewer's ambition, and an appreciation of writers like Klaus Rittland, Hermine Villinger, Charlotte Niese, Elsbeth Meyer-Förster, Richard Nordmann, etc., or even the terse and forceful Ilse Frapan, would neither have affected the general estimate nor made a perceptible change in the line of development as traced. The same consideration justifies the omission of Bertha von Suttner's *Die Waffen nieder!* ("Down with Arms!"), which owes the international applause bestowed upon it solely to its humane sentiment. The book, it will be remembered, is a plea for general disarmament. Its literary value is slight. The chronological limit of the theme precludes more than passing reference to the so-called "Vera" literature, which has rapidly crystallized round the recent anonymous diary of a young Viennese girl who announces herself in the title, *Eine für Viele* ("One for Many") as the spokeswoman of a numerous class; to the Baroness von Heyking's *Briefe, die ihn nicht erreichten* (" Letters that did not reach him "), and many other books. It may be of some interest to know that Ernst Georgy's *Die Berliner Range* (" The Berlin Hobbledehoy "), a phenomenally popular series of cheap-grade fun-books, comes from the pen of a woman.

The writers here considered have been, with very few exceptions, novelists. This is natural enough, since in the field of the prose epic, which throughout the nineteenth century has been the most diligently worked of all literary fields, the authoresses have, as a rule, exercised their talents. In the other literary genera they have produced relatively little that counts for much in the history of literature. Lyrists we have in plenty, and a number of them are worthy of praise, as, for instance, Anna Ritter, Agnes Miegel, Mia Holm, Alberta von Puttkamer, Thekla Lingen, etc. But, outside of the women lyrists who have been discussed, it would be difficult to mention any whose verse rings full and true, and sounds the note of a deep poetic conscientiousness. Certainly we cannot pay this tribute to Johanna Ambrosius, about whose sympathetic songs so much ado has been made. She is a plain, sensible peasant woman whom Professor Weiss-Schrattenthal, the benevolent patron of aspiring authoresses, had the questionable taste to dress out as a species of German Sappho and to have presented to the public by her East Prussian countryman Sudermann. Thirty-six editions of her poems were exhausted in four years, yet even that phenomenal book-trade success will not keep her memory alive. Ambrosius has clearly been overrated. She has opened to view a soul-life of great depth, but of inconsiderable compass. And she is too well read in devotional books and family magazines to have preserved the refreshing spontaneity of a genuine singer of the people. Lyric qualities of a much higher order belong to Marie Madeleine, who is unfortunately the most brazenly unabashed of all modern verse writers.

In the province of the drama the successors of Birch-Pfeiffer have not made many brilliant conquests. Of living women dramatists, Elsa

Bernstein, who writes under the assumed name Ernst Rosmer, is the only one who has won real distinction. The singularly happy combination of realism and romanticism in her fairy piece, *Die Königskinder* ("The Royal Children") (1895), has done much to establish the reign of the *Märchendrama* ushered in by Hauptmann and Fulda.

On the whole, women have shown a certain ineptitude, or it may be only a reluctance, to essay literature under the restrictions of definite form, and have exhibited a leaning towards the less exacting prose narrative. And, as a class, women novelists have their pronounced failings. They are found lacking in the calm objectiveness that flows from historic consciousness, and in a well-balanced sense of personality. Likewise, we feel strongly, in their interpretation of detached facts of life, the absence of a controlling philosophy; simple truths they grasp quickly enough, but too readily erect them uncemented into a system.

I have not been able to speak of the German authoress of the nineteenth century with full-blown eulogy. However, the reader has not failed to observe in her story the marks of an up-grade movement calculated to disarm the pessimist. It is certainly a fact from which women ambitious for their sex may derive much gratification, that one cannot name the foremost living writers of Germany without including several women.

And as for the vexed problem that springs into view every time the woman question comes up in literary criticism: Is woman excluded by natural limitations from the higher realms of creative art? I might answer: Ricarda Huch! . . . to be told, probably, that one swallow does not make a summer. So again, as at the outset, I ask permission to leave the question open. It was not the object of this sketch to prove a thesis, but rather to trace a development, and to describe the resultant situation.

INDEX

By PAUL REIFF, Ph.D.

Instructor in German, Washington University